A Young Astronomer's Guide to the Night Sky

This is for you, Barb. I couldn't have done it without you!

A Young Astronomer's Guide to the Night Sky

Michael R. Porcellino

TAB BOOKS
Blue Ridge Summit, PA

FIRST EDITION
FIRST PRINTING

© 1991 by **TAB BOOKS**
TAB BOOKS is a division of McGraw-Hill, Inc.

Library of Congress Cataloging-in-Publication Data

Porcellino, Michael R.
    Young astronomer's guide to the night sky / by Michael R. Porcellino.
        p.   cm.
    Includes bibliographical references and index.
    Summary: Introduces the stars according to the seasons of the year, using history, mythology, and projects involving very little optical aid.
    ISBN 0-8306-7495-0   ISBN 0-8306-3495-9 (pbk.)
    1. Constellations—Observers' manuals—Juvenile literature.
2. Astronomy—Observers' manuals—Juvenile literature.
[1. Constellations—Observers' manuals. 2. Astronomy—Observers' manuals. 3. Stars—Observers' manuals.] I. Title.
QB63.P593   1990
523.8′022′3—dc20   90-43541
                                          CIP
                                          AC

TAB BOOKS offers software for sale. For information and a catalog, please contact TAB Software Department, Blue Ridge Summit, PA 17294-0850.

Questions regarding the content of this book should be addressed to:

    Reader Inquiry Branch
    TAB BOOKS
    Blue Ridge Summit, PA 17294-0214

Acquisitons Editor: Roland S. Phelps
Book Editor: Andrew Yoder
Production: Katherine G. Brown
Cover photograph courtesy of Susan Riley, Harrisonburg, Va.

Contents

Introduction   ix

Acknowlegments   xi

1 Figures in the Sky   1
Asterisms and Constellations *1*
Today's Constellations *5*
The Name Game *9*

2 Celestial Conundrums   11
How Does the Sky Move? *11*
How Bright Are the Stars? *16*
How Far Is That Star? *18*
How Are Distances Measured in Space? *18*

3 Equipment for Skywatching   21
Seeing in the Dark *21*
Aiding the Eye *23*
Portable Skies *25*
Your Observing Notebook *29*

4 Stars That Never Set   31
Ursa Major *32*
Ursa Minor *34*
Camelopardalis *35*
Draco *35*
Cassiopeia *36*
Cepheus *36*
A Project for the Young Astronomer *37*

5 The Brilliant Sky of Winter   39

Taurus   *39*
Auriga   *45*
Orion   *46*
Gemini   *48*
Canis Major   *50*
Canis Minor   *52*
Eridanus   *52*
Lepus   *52*
Monoceros   *53*
Puppis   *53*
Columba   *53*
Caelum   *53*
A Project for the Young Astronomer   *53*

6 Harbingers of Spring   55

Lynx   *55*
Cancer   *55*
Hydra   *58*
Leo   *58*
Leo Minor   *58*
Sextans   *58*
Canes Venatici   *58*
Coma Bernices   *58*
Virgo   *59*
Crater   *62*
Corvus   *62*
Pyxis   *64*
Antlia   *64*
Centaurus   *64*
A Project for the Young Astronomer   *64*

7 Keystones and Scorpions   67

Bootes   *67*
Corona Borealis   *69*
Hercules   *69*
Scorpius   *71*
Corona Australis   *71*
Libra   *72*
Lupus   *72*
Serpens and Ophiuchus   *72*
A Project for the Young Astronomer   *73*

8 Around the Summer Triangle   75

Lyra 75
Cygnus 78
Vulpecula 78
Aquila 81
Scutum 81
Sagitta 81
Delphinus 81
Sagittarius 81
Capricornus 81
A Project for the Young Astronomer 85

9 Stars for an Autumn Evening   87

Aquarius 87
Pisces Austrinus 89
Lacerta 89
Equuleus 89
Sculptor 90
Andromeda 90
Cetus 91
Fornax 94
Aries 94
Triangulum 94
Perseus 94
Pegasus 97
Pisces 98
A Project for the Young Astronomer 98

10 The Southern Stars   101

Apus 102
Ara 102
Carina 103
Chameleon 103
Circinus 103
Crux 103
Dorado 103
Grus 103
Horologium 104
Hyrdus 104
Indus 104
Mensa 104
Microscopium 105

Musca   *105*
Norma   *105*
Octans   *105*
Pavo   *105*
Phoenix   *105*
Pictor   *105*
Reticulum   *105*
Telescopium   *106*
Triangulum Australe   *106*
Tucana   *106*
Vela   *106*
Volans   *106*

11 The Beacon of the Night   **107**
Phases   *107*
Craters and Seas   *110*
A Project for the Young Astronomer   *111*

12 The Family of the Sun   **119**
Mercury   *119*
Venus   *121*
Mars   *123*
Jupiter   *125*
Saturn   *127*
Uranus   *127*
Neptune   *128*
Pluto   *129*
Comets and Meteors   *129*

Glossary   **133**

Suggested Reading   **137**

Index   **139**

Introduction

*I*t is hard to believe that the night sky was once studied with nothing more than the human eye and mind. For thousands of years, people could only look at the stars, ask questions, and wonder. Then, in 1609, Galileo turned his newly built *optik tube* toward the heavens and the way we studied the night sky changed.

Today, we live in an age of huge telescopes. On Earth, telescopes probe the night sky with computer-controlled equipment that can detect the light from a match on the other side of the world. The Hubble Space Telescope, launched in 1990, will give us views of the universe that were impossible a few years ago. Today's astronomy is a combination of computer chips and telescopes that extend our vision to the edge of time and space.

Unfortunately, in this clutter of computers, telescopes, and spacecraft, people have lost sight of the beauty of the night sky. To many here on Earth, the stars are nothing more than tiny, feeble lights in the night sky—if they can see them at all. They forget that each star in the sky is an individual. The light from these stars can tell us much about those individuals, but looking so closely at them causes us to miss their real beauty. Above the glow of the powerful streetlights that illuminate our cities, there is an entire universe waiting to be discovered if we will only take the time to do so.

I had two goals in mind when I sat down to write *A YOUNG ASTRONOMER'S GUIDE TO THE NIGHT SKY*. First, I wanted to introduce you to the night sky. The darkened dome of the night sky can be a wonderful place, but you have to know your way around. The stars can seem confusing at first, but the more you watch their nightly parade, the more comfortable you will feel among them. Second, I wanted to share with you some of the secrets of the stars. The sky and the stars were studied for thousands of years before the telescope was invented. The sky that rolls over our heads is the same sky that the peoples of ancient Greece and Rome gazed upon. It is the same sky that amazed the Mayans, the Arabs, and the Chinese.

Now we can look at the same sky with knowledge that has come from the largest telescopes ever built. We can see the sky with different eyes—with eyes that see the wonders that the ancients gazed upon, but tuned into the reality of what we are seeing. To the ancients, for example, the glow at the tip of Orion's sword was a "cloud" that they could not explain. Today we know that it is indeed a cloud, but unlike any cloud that floats in our skies. It is a cloud of gas and dust; and inside that cloud, stars are being born.

In this book, I've tried to group the constellations together in manageable bites. I hope this approach gives you an idea of how those individual constellations relate to each other. I've also listed brief descriptions for each constellation and how you can find them in the sky. Finally, you will find out a little about the universe in which we live. Many of the constellations listed here have a little piece of astronomical history within its borders. You will learn, for example, about double stars in the section on Ursa Major, about nebulae in the section on Orion, and about how stars die in the section on Lyra. In addition to a guide to the sky, this book will be your guide to finding out what we have discovered in our never-ending quest to learn about our universe.

Many people think that you need a powerful telescope to study the night sky, but you don't. To this end, I have included fifteen projects that you can undertake, most using nothing more than your unaided eyes. You can discover star colors, hunt for Venus during the daytime, or try to identify features on the Moon, all with the unaided eye. Some of the projects will require some optical aid, but nothing more than a good pair of binoculars. I hope you enjoy working on these projects and I would like to know how you completed them.

The magic and beauty of the starry night belongs to anyone who wants to take the time to look up. All that is really needed are clear skies, your own eyes, and a guide to what is up there. I hope that this book will be your guide to the night sky and will start you on a lifetime of wonder at the beauty that lies just above our heads.

Clear skies, my friends!

Acknowledgments

I want to thank everyone who helped in making this book possible: Sue Cosentino for her illustrations. Pat Shand and Lick Observatory for some of the photos. NASA for their photos. The folks at the Adler Planetarium library for use of their fine collection of books. Dan Joyce, Tim Phillip, Jim Carroll and the rest of the C.A.S. for their input. Mark Stauffer, Barb Lux, and Lee Keith for their help, comments and photos. And, of course, Roland Phelps of TAB for putting up with me.

Chapter 1

Figures in the sky

*H*umans have always seen figures in the stars. Just which culture first used the night sky as a giant blackboard to record their legends and heroes is unknown. From information uncovered by archaeologists, we do know that almost every ancient civilization drew star figures in the sky.

The cultures that grew up along the shores of the great rivers—the Nile, Tigris, and Euphrates—all used the stars to form the figures of things that held special significance to them. With a few exceptions, the kinds of figures and the reason they were special have been lost over the course of time. Egyptian scrolls speak of star figures with names like the lion, the hare, and the hippopotamus, but there is no record of where in the sky these figures can be found. Clay tablets found noting property boundaries in Babylon carry what seem to be outlines of star figures, but again, their exact meaning has been lost.

The constellations we recognize today come primarily from the Greeks. Throughout their history, they created wonderful stories and illustrated them in the sky: The stories of Hercules and his twelve labors; Perseus and his quest to save the beautiful Andromeda from the sea monster Cetus; and the great hunter, Orion, with his hunting dogs, Canis Major and Canis Minor. Greek storytellers outlined their tales in the stars over 3,000 years ago, and you can still see them in the night sky (see FIG. 1-1).

ASTERISMS AND CONSTELLATIONS

The first time you look at the night sky, you will notice that the stars are not spread around evenly. In some places, stars are strewn thick and bright, like tiny diamonds on a velvet black cloth. In other areas of the sky, you are able to see few, if any, stars.

1-1 The astronomers and storytellers of Greece imagined the constellations looked like this. (A) Taurus, (B) Hercules, (C)Perseus, (D)Leo.

Susan D. Cosentino

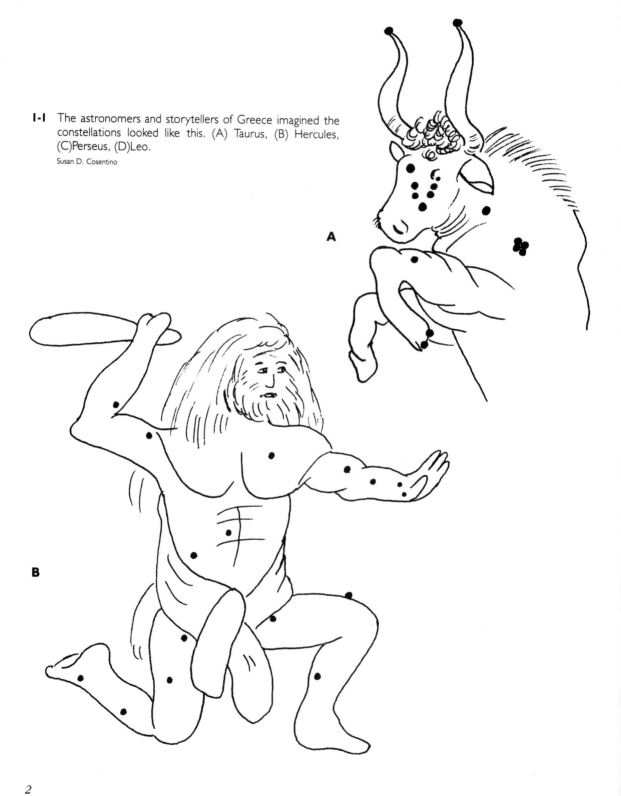

I-I Cont.

C

D

Look carefully at groups of stars and you might see distinctive shapes. It's like playing a celestial game of "connect the dots." Groups of stars that take on an easily recognized shape or form are called *asterisms*.

The Big Dipper (see FIG. 1-2) is a good example of an asterism. The seven stars that make up the Dipper are bright, easy to recognize, and form a distinct shape. Four stars make up the "bowl" and three stars form the "handle."

The peoples of the ancient world looked at the groups of stars and played their own game of connect the dots. They used the dome of the sky like a drawing board. They created the figures of their greatest heroes in the stars and told stories of their exploits in the sky.

Today, these star figures are called *constellations*. A constellation is a basic asterism plus much more of the surrounding sky and stars. Being able to pick out an asterism within a much larger constellation makes it easier for you to find the constellation itself. The asterism we call the Big Dipper is part of the much larger constellation called *Ursa Major*, the Great Bear. As you can see in FIG. 1-3, the constellation contains much more celestial real estate than the easily visible asterism.

Look at the sky with your imagination as well as your eyes. What shapes can you see in the stars? You might see a lopsided box, a triangle, an arrow, or a large cross. Use the star groups in FIG. 1-4 and see what asterisms you can find in them. Learning to find asterisms will enable you to become familiar with the constellations and find your way around the night sky easily.

In many cases, the asterisms we see are the result of a random alignment of stars as seen from Earth. The constellations in tonight's sky are much different from the constellations that blazed in the heavens 100,000 years ago. The constellations that will light the night sky in another 100,000 years will be different from the ones you see tonight.

This change occurs because the stars move through space. The stars that create some star figures are moving in random directions and are

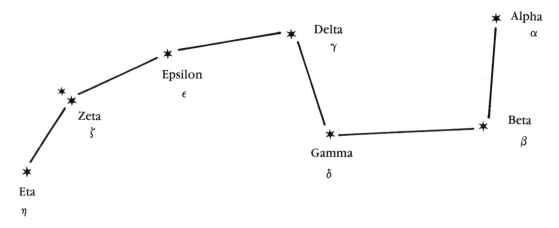

1-2 The asterism known as the Big Dipper.

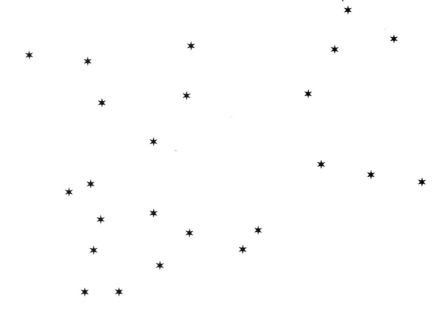

1-3 The Big Dipper and the rest of Ursa Major.

totally unrelated to each other. These stars are ''strangers'' passing in the night sky and, for a brief instant (brief on the cosmic scale of time) we see them form a constellation. Other star figures are made up of stars that are actually related to each other. They move through space in the same direction and have what astronomers call the same *proper motion*.

The stories that follow constellations vary from culture to culture, but many of them are surprisingly similar. For example, many of the legends that surround the Big Dipper and the constellation Ursa Major have something to do with bears. The Greeks tell the story of a young man and his mother who were changed into bears by the gods. The mother became the Great Bear and the son became the Little Bear. Many North American Indian tribes saw a bear (the ''bowl'' of the dipper) chased by three hunters (the three stars of the ''handle'' of the dipper). These cultures, widely separated by time and distance, saw similar things in the star figure that we call the ''Big Dipper.''

TODAY'S CONSTELLATIONS

Over the centuries, star mappers have included as many as 106 constellations in their star charts. Many of these ''constellations,'' especially those in the southern sky, consisted of nothing more than a few dim stars. Many people who drew sky charts would create ''constellations'' to honor their friends or benefactors, and in some cases, a constellation would carry three or four names. It became so confusing that in 1930 members of the

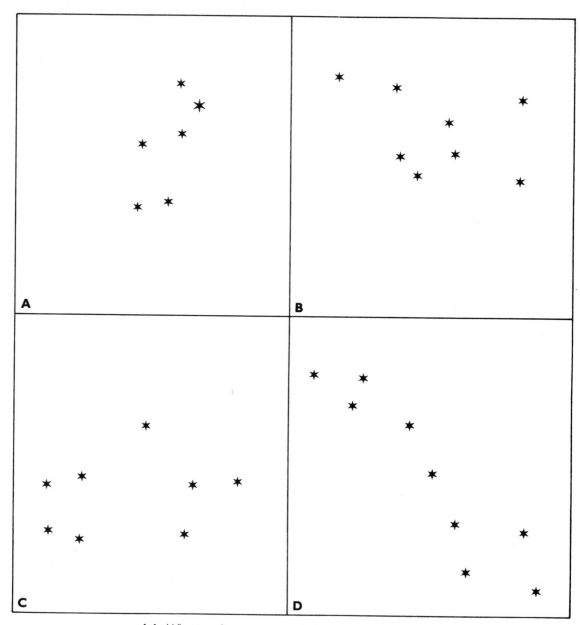

1-4 What asterisms can you make from these star groups?

International Astronomical Union (IAU), a society of professional astronomers, had to call a special meeting to decide which constellations they would recognize as legitimate.

The astronomers picked the 88 "official" constellations that we recognize today (see TABLE 1-1). Of these, 55 are visible from the continental United States in their complete or almost complete forms. The northern

Table 1-1 The 88 Constellations.

Astronomical Name	Common Name	Abbreviation
Andromeda	The chained lady	AND
Antilia	The pump	ANT
Apus	Bird of paradise	APS[2]
Aquarius	The water bearer	AQR
Aquila	The eagle	AQL
Ara	The altar	ARA[2]
Aries	The ram	ARI
Auriga	The charioteer	AUR
Bootes	The herdsman	BOO
Caelum	The chisel	CAE[1]
Camelopardalis	The giraffe	CAM
Cancer	The crab	CNC
Canes Venatici	The hunting dogs	CVn
Canis major	The greater dog	CMa
Canis minor	The lesser dog	CMi
Capricornus	The goat	CAP
Carina	The keel	CAR[2]
Cassiopeia	The queen	CAS
Centaurus	The centaur	CEN[1]
Cepheus	The king	CEP
Cetus	The whale	CET
Chamaeleon	The chameleon	CHA[2]
Circinus	The compass	CIR[2]
Columba	The dove	COL[1]
Coma Bernices	Bernice's hair	COM
Corona Australis	The southern crown	CrA[1]
Corona Borealis	The northern crown	CrB
Corvus	The crow	CRV
Crater	The cup	CRT
Crux	The southern cross	CRU[2]
Cygnus	The swan	CYG
Delphinus	The dolphin	DEL
Dorado	The swordfish	DOR[2]
Draco	The dragon	DRA
Equuleus	The little horse	EQU
Eridanus	The river	ERI[1]
Fornax	The furnace	FOR
Gemini	The twins	GEM
Grus	The crane	GRU[1]
Hercules	Hercules	HER
Horologium	The clock	HOR[2]

Table I-I Cont.

Astronomical Name	Common Name	Abbreviation
Hydra	The sea monster	HYA
Hydrus	The water snake	HYI[2]
Indus	The indian	IND[2]
Lacerta	The lizard	LAC
Leo	The lion	LEO
Leo Minor	The little lion	LMi
Lepus	The hare	LEP
Libra	The scale	LIB
Lupus	The wolf	LUP[1]
Lynx	The lynx	LYN
Lyra	The harp	LYR
Mensa	The table	MEN[2]
Microscopium	The microscope	MIC[1]
Monoceros	The unicorn	MON
Musca	The fly	MUS[2]
Norma	The level	NOR[2]
Octans	The octant	OCT[2]
Ophiuchus	The snake bearer	OPH
Orion	The hunter	ORI
Pavo	The peacock	PAV[2]
Pegasus	The winged horse	PEG
Perseus	The hero	PER
Phoenix	The phoenix	PHE[2]
Pictor	The easel	PIC[2]
Pisces	The fish	PSC
Pisces Austrinus	The southern fish	PsA
Puppis	The stern	PUP[1]
Pyxis	The ship's compass	PYX[1]
Reticulum	The net	RET[2]
Sagitta	The arrow	SGE
Sagittarius	The archer	SGR
Scorpius	The scorpion	SCO
Sculptor	The sculptor	SCL
Scutum	The shield	SCT
Serpens	The serpent	SER
Sextans	The sextant	SEX
Taurus	The bull	TAU
Telescopium	The telescope	TEL[2]
Triangulum	The triangle	TRI
Triangulum Australe	Southern triangle	TrA[2]
Tucana	The toucan	TUC[2]
Ursa Major	The greater bear	UMa
Ursa Minor	The lesser bear	UMi

Table 1-1   Cont.

Astronomical Name	Common Name	Abbreviation
Vela	The sails	VEL[2]
Virgo	The virgin	VIR
Volans	The flying fish	VOL[2]
Vulpecula	The fox	VUL

1. Only part of these constellations can be seen from 42° north.
2. These constellations can only be seen from the southern hemisphere.

sections of ten more are also visible from the United States, but 23 are visible only from the Southern Hemisphere.

Most of the constellations in our skies still have the names given to them by the Greek astronomers. A few, those visible in the Southern Hemisphere, retain the "modern" names given to them in the 1800s.

THE NAME GAME

Each star visible to the unaided eye has a name. Some stars even have more than one name, so it can get a bit confusing for someone trying to learn the stars of the night sky.

The system used for naming the stars goes back to 1603. Johann Bayer, a German astronomer, started to list stars with a Greek letter (see TABLE 1-2) and a form of the Latin name of the constellation to which they belong. This combination makes for such strange-sounding monikers as Alpha Cygni, Gamma Delphini, and Alpha Aquilae. You might notice that

Table 1-2   The Greek Alphabet.

Alpha	α	Iota	ι	Rho	ϱ
Beta	β	Kappa	$\varkappa$	Sigma	σ
Gamma	γ	Lambda	λ	Tau	τ
Delta	δ	Mu	μ	Upsilon	υ
Epsilon	ϵ	Nu	ν	Phi	ϕ
Zeta	ζ	Xi	ξ	Chi	χ
Eta	η	Omicron	o	Psi	ψ
Theta	θ	Pi	π	Omega	ω

the name of the constellation itself is slightly different from the constellation name when used to identify stars. This style is called the *genitive* or *possessive case* of the constellation name.

The stars in a particular constellation are assigned a Greek letter according to their brightness. The brightest star is designated Alpha (α), the first letter of the Greek alphabet, and the others are named in their descending order of brightness. Beta (β) is the second brightest star, Gamma (γ) is the third, and so on. Using this system, the brightest star in Perseus is *Alpha Persei*, the second brightest is *Beta Persei*, etc. This system continues until the constellation either runs of stars or the alphabet runs out of letters.

Table 1-3 The Brightest Stars.

Name	Cons	Mag.	Transit
Sirius	Alpha CMa	− 1.4	FEB
Canopus	Alpha CAR	−0.7	NOT VIS
Rigel Kent	Alpha CEN	−0.1	NOT VIS
Arcturus	Alpha BOO	−0.06	JUL
Vega	Alpha LYR	0.03	AUG
Rigel	Beta ORI	0.08	JAN
Capella	Alpha AUR	0.09	JAN
Procyon	Alpha CMi	0.3	MAR
Achernar	Alpha ERI	0.49	NOT VIS
Hadar	Beta CEN	0.61	NOT VIS
Altair	Alpha AQL	0.75	SEP
Aldebaran	Alpha TAU	0.78	JAN
Acrux	Alpha CRU	0.8	NOT VIS
Betelgeuse	Alpha ORI	0.85	FEB
Antares	Alpha SCO	0.92	JUL
Spica	Alpha VIR	0.98	MAY
Pollux	Beta GEM	1.15	MAR
Fomalhaut	Alpha PsA	1.16	OCT
Deneb	Alpha CYG	1.26	SEP
Mimosa	Beta CRU	1.28	NOT VIS
Regulus	Alpha LEO	1.33	APR

Stars listed as NOT VIS are not visible from most of the continental United States.

In most cases, the astronomers who assigned star names ran out of Greek letters long before they ran out of stars. When this happened, the remaining stars were given small Roman letters (a, b, c . . . z) until these ran out. So, some stars are labeled, for example, g Herculis or f Hydrae.

In 1725, John Flamsteed began assigning stars ordinary numbers. These *Flamsteed numbers* begin at the western border of the constellation with number 1 and move eastward. Today, astronomers refer to many fainter stars by their Flamsteed number and the genitive form of the constellation name, for example, 70 Ophiuchi, 61 Cygni, and 7 Tauri.

Many stars have been given proper names in addition to their letter designations. The brightest stars (see TABLE 1-3) also have their own proper names, as do many of the other stars we can see. Alpha Ursae Minoris is better known as *Polaris*; Beta Cygni, one of the sky's most beautiful double stars, is commonly called *Albireo*; and the first variable star to be discovered, Omicron Ceti, is called *Mira*.

Chapter 2

Celestial conundrums

*M*any things in the night sky can appear puzzling to the new observer. The way the sky seems to move, the different brightnesses of the stars, and the vast distances involved can confuse anyone.

HOW DOES THE SKY MOVE?

If you go out any night of the year and watch the constellations for about an hour, you will notice that they seem to move across the sky. The stars all appear to rise in the east and set in the west. The ancients saw this motion and assumed that the stars moved around the Earth. Because of this motion, they thought the Earth was the center of the universe.

However, this motion is only an illusion caused by the Earth's rotation on its axis, called *apparent motion*. We observe the starry sky from a moving platform, the Earth. The Earth turns on its axis from west to east, so the stars only appear to move across the sky from east to west (see FIG. 2-1).

If you look carefully at the stars, you will see that all but one appear to have this motion. Hanging motionless in the northern sky is a point around which all the stars appear to rotate (FIG. 2-2). That point is called the *North Celestial Pole* (NCP). If we extend the axis of the Earth into space, it would point to a spot in the constellation of Ursa Minor, the Little Bear (FIG. 2-3). Near this point is a relatively bright star called *Polaris*. Polaris marks the NCP for us today, but it was not always the Pole star.

If we could watch the Earth move around the Sun from a point out in space, we would see something interesting. As the Earth revolves around the Sun, it wobbles like a top. This wobble is called *precession*, and it causes the NCP, as we see it from Earth, to slowly move in a circle against the background stars (see FIG. 2-4). It takes the Earth 26,000 years to complete one wobble. In that period of time, the apparent NCP will change.

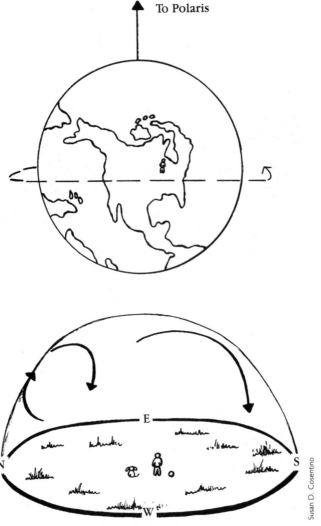

2-1 How the Earth and sky move.

When the pyramids of Egypt were being excavated, archaeologists discovered a shaft in the wall of the Great Pyramid that seemed to point to an empty spot in the sky. After much puzzlement, astronomers and archaeologists realized that when the pyramid was built about 3000 years ago, the star Thuban in the constellation Draco marked the NCP. The pyramid shafts were aligned with this star and the nearby NCP. Today, Polaris is closest to the NCP. In 14,000 years, Vega, the fourth brightest star in the sky and the brightest star in the constellation Lyra, will be the nearest star to the NCP.

The position of Polaris shows you *latitude*, how far north of the equator you are located. The distance of Polaris above your northern

2-2 A time-exposure photograph shows that stars move across the sky. (A) Stars near the north celestial pole move in ever tighter circles as you near Polaris. (B) Stars farther away from Polaris, at the celestial equator move in straighter lines.

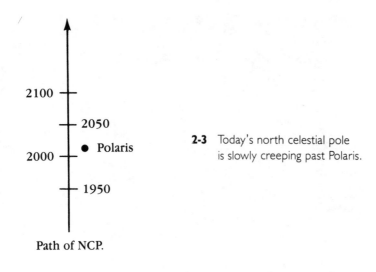

2-3 Today's north celestial pole is slowly creeping past Polaris.

Path of NCP.

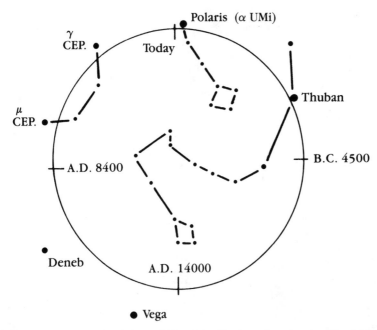

2-4 Precession is the track of the wobble of the Earth against the sky. The NCP of 3000 B.C. was near Thuban; today's is near Polaris. In A.D. 14,000 it will be near Vega.

horizon is equal to your latitude (see FIG. 2-5). The farther south you live, the lower in the northern sky Polaris will appear; the farther north you live, the higher in the sky it will appear. For example, if you live in Chicago, Polaris will appear to be 42 degrees above the northern horizon. You can look at an atlas of the United States and find the latitude line for

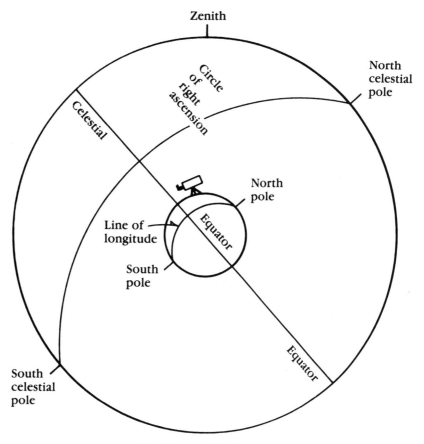

2-5 The celestial sphere.

your city along the edge of the map. What is your latitude? How far above the northern horizon will Polaris appear from where you observe?

Astronomers also use the Earth's equator to help find their way around the sky. They project an imaginary line into the sky that extends the Earth's equator into space. You can find this *celestial equator* by subtracting your latitude from 90 degrees. The result will show you how far above the southern horizon the celestial equator is located. In Chicago, for example, the celestial equator is about 48 degrees above the southern horizon. How far above the southern horizon is the celestial equator at your observing site?

It's easy to work out these numbers on a piece of paper, but how can you see if your answers hold true for what is in the sky? The answer is literally right in your hand. It is your hand! Hold your arm out to its full length, then extend your little finger. The tip of this finger covers about 1 degree of sky. The full Moon is about 1/2 degree across, so you should be able to cover it with your finger. Try it and see if it works.

Your closed fist covers 10 degrees, and the distance between your outstretched little finger and thumb covers 20 degrees. Does it work? Maybe the little finger was a lucky guess! Go out tonight and try it. Measure the distance between the northern horizon and Polaris. How close was your paper calculation to the actual measurement (see FIG. 2-6)?

This method works because, although every person is different in size, the relationship between arm length and hand size remains constant. Your fist, held at arm's length, will cover 10 degrees of sky whether you are 6 feet tall or 4 feet 10 inches tall. This method remains constant whether you are 10 or 50 years old. You hold the key to exploring the sky in your hand!

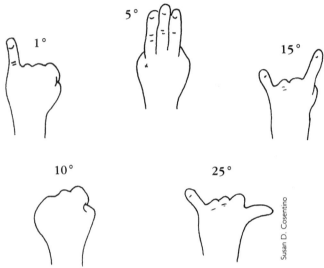

2-6 Holding your hand at arm's length translates to these measures.

HOW BRIGHT ARE THE STARS?

When you begin your tour of the night sky, you will quickly notice that stars do not all have the same brightness. The brightness of a star is measured on a scale called the *magnitude scale*. On this scale, the higher the number, the fainter the star; the lower the number, the brighter the star.

The magnitude scale that is used today was developed by the Greek astronomer Hipparchus of Rhodes. In 135 B.C., Hipparchus became the first astronomer to list all the stars according to their brightnesses. The brightest stars on his original list were called *first-magnitude stars*. Slightly fainter stars were called *second-magnitude stars*. Stars fainter than second magnitude were called *third-magnitude* and so on, down to the dimmest stars he could see.

Today, the magnitude scale is like the original scale developed by Hipparchus, but much improved. We have kept the magnitude listings that he used, but astronomers no longer rely on estimates made by eye for determining the magnitude of a star. *Photoelectric photometers* can determine star magnitudes with much greater accuracy. The scale itself, which Hipparchus started at first magnitude and ended at sixth magnitude, has been greatly extended. Today's telescopes can detect stars that have a magnitude of 28!

Astronomers learned that the brightest of Hipparchus' stars, those of the first magnitude, included some that were actually brighter than first magnitude. Of the 15 stars that Hipparchus classified as first magnitude, modern photoelectric photometers found that none were exactly first magnitude, and four were bright enough to have their own magnitude classes. So astronomers created zero magnitude for the bright stars Capella and Vega. The remaining two stars, Arcturus and Sirius, are so bright that their magnitudes are given a minus sign to indicate their great brilliancy. Astronomers have also assigned magnitudes to the two brightest objects in our sky, the Moon and the Sun. The sun has a magnitude of −26, and the Full Moon has a magnitude of −12 (see TABLE 2-1).

Table 2-1   The Visual Magnitude Scale.

Name	MAG.
Sun	−26
Full Moon	−12
Venus	−4
Jupiter	−2
Sirius	−1.4
Spica	+1.0
Naked eye limit	+6.0
7 × 50 binocular limit	+10
6-inch telescope limit	+13
200-inch telescope limit	+22

One thing that astronomers changed from the Hipparchus magnitude scale was the difference between magnitudes. Each change of one magnitude increases or decreases the brightness of a star 2.5 times. To determine the magnitude difference between two stars, multiply the magnitude differences. A first-magnitude star is 2.5 times brighter than a second-magnitude star, the former is but 2.5 times fainter than a zero-magnitude star. A first-magnitude star is 6.25 times (2.5 × 2.5) brighter than a third-magnitude star. The difference between a first-magnitude star and the faintest stars we can see with the unaided eye (sixth-magnitude) is 100 (2.5 × 2.5 × 2.5 × 2.5 × 2.5), so the sixth-magnitude star is 100 times fainter than the first-magnitude star. The difference between the brightest object in the sky, the Sun at magnitude −26, and the dimmest star visible to your unaided eye, is 33 magnitudes. However, if you multiply the difference between each magnitude (2.5 × 2.5, 33 times), you will find that the Sun is over 100 trillion times brighter than the sixth-magnitude star!

HOW FAR IS THAT STAR?

You know how far you live from your friend's house and how long it takes to reach there from home. Your friend might live 5 miles away and it takes 15 minutes to get there on the bus. You measure the distance in terms of miles and the travel time in miles per hour.

Distances in space are so great that they cannot be measured in miles. Astronomers measure these vast distances by using the only suitable way they have, the *speed of light*, which is the ultimate speed limit of the universe. At 186,000 miles per second, the light that warms us on the Earth takes 8 minutes to arrive from the Sun, and it is relatively close to us at 93 million miles away.

The distance to the nearest star system, Alpha Centauri, is over 24 trillion miles. Even at 186,000 miles per second, it takes light over four years to reach us from Alpha Centauri. The distance traveled by light in 1 year is called a *light-year* and covers almost 6 trillion miles! Table 2-2 lists some of the nearest stars.

Table 2-2 Some of the Nearest Stars.

Name	CONS	MAG.	Distance
Sun	———	−26	8 light minutes
*Alpha Centauri	Centaurus	−0.1	4.3 light years
Barnard's Star	Ophiuchus	+9.5	6.0 light years
*Sirius	Canis Major	−1.4	8.9 light years
Epsilon Eridani	Eridanus	+3.7	10.8 light years
*61 Cygni	Cygnus	+5.2	11.1 light years
*Procyon	Canis Minor	+0.3	11.4 light years
Tau Ceti	Cetus	+3.5	11.8 light years
*Omicron-2 Eridani	Eridanus	+4.4	15.7 light years
*70 Ophiuchi	Ophiuchus	+4.2	16.1 light years
Altair	Aquila	+0.7	16.5 light years
*Eta Cassiopeiae	Cassiopeia	+3.5	18.0 light years

Stars listed with an asterisk (*) are multiple star systems.

The Sun, Earth, and other members of the Solar System are located in the Milky Way galaxy. The Milky Way is a huge collection of stars numbering in the hundreds of billions. Each of the stars that we can see in the night sky is a member of this galaxy. If you could look down on our galaxy, you would see a great spiral-shaped lens of stars almost 100,000 light-years across. At the center is a huge, bright, star-filled core with "arms" of gas, dust, and more stars spinning away from the center. We are located in one of the arms, about 30,000 light-years from the center of the galaxy.

HOW ARE DISTANCES MEASURED IN SPACE?

The Greek astronomers were very inventive when confronted with a problem. It is commonly believed that prior to Columbus's voyage, everyone thought that the world was flat. However, the Greeks in 450 B.C., saw the shadow the Earth cast on the moon during a lunar eclipse.

They noticed that the edge of the shadow was curved, not straight, as they would expect if the Earth was flat. When they combined this observation with the fact that at noon the Sun appeared to be at different heights above the horizon for observers at different locations, they deduced that the Earth was a sphere. They then determined that the spherical Earth was about 8000 miles in diameter (compared to today's figure of 7920 miles) and 25,000 miles in circumference (compared to today's figure of 24,902 miles). These estimates were very accurate considering that they were working with sticks and shadows!

The Greek astronomers next turned to finding the size of and distance to the Moon. Using their dimensions of the Earth, they applied geometry to the problem. They again used the size of the Earth's shadow during a lunar eclipse and were able to come up with a distance of 240,000 miles (compared to today's figure of 238,000 miles) and a diameter of about 2160 miles for the Moon (right on the money!).

However, when they tried to apply their techniques to finding the distance to the Sun and stars, they fell far short. Greek astronomers determined that the Sun was 5 million miles from Earth, and they could not even begin to appreciate the distances to the stars!

The method used by astronomers to determine the distance to a star is called *parallax*. You can see how it works by holding a pencil at arm's length. If you look at the pencil with one eye open, you will see it against a background of familiar objects. Close that eye and open the other, and you will see the pencil shift against the background. This shift can be measured to show how far the pencil is from you. Astronomers can use the same technique on a much larger scale to measure the distances to the planets and stars.

The important thing in measuring with parallax is having a "baseline" large enough to show you the shift of the object against the background. With the pencil experiment, the baseline is the distance between your eyes. This small baseline works fine for objects that are very close, but it won't work with the planets or stars.

To determine the distance to the planets, astronomers used the Earth itself to provide a "baseline" 8000 miles across. Two astronomers, at opposite points on the Earth, recorded the position of a planet against the background stars at exactly the same time. They then measured the amount of shift between the two measurements and were able to calculate how far the planet was from the Earth.

When they tried to apply this method to determine the distances to the stars, the astronomers found that they needed a much larger baseline. In order to get this larger baseline, they decided to use the orbit of the Earth. They then made two detailed observations of the target star and its surrounding star field—not at the same time, but six months apart. In that time, the Earth would carry the observer in its orbit so that the two observations were separated by 186 million miles. Astronomers were astounded by their findings. Very few stars moved against the background star fields, even when this gigantic baseline was used. The parallax shift of the few stars that did move was extremely small.

Chapter 3

Equipment
for skywatching

*M*any people think that in order to study the sky you need a large telescope. Don't let 'em fool ya! Nothing could be further from the truth! All you need are clear skies, your eyes, and a place to relax under the stars! Before Galileo came along and pointed his optik tube skyward, everything in astronomy was done with the human eye.

Tycho Brahe (1546-1601) did quite a bit with the unaided eye. He recorded star and planetary positions with such accuracy that Johann Kepler (1571-1630) used this data to figure out how the planets moved around the Sun and formulate his three laws of planetary motion (see FIG. 3-1).

SEEING IN THE DARK

The basic instrument of the astronomer is the eye. Everything else— binoculars, telescopes, even spacecraft—is only an extension of the eye.

Your eye is a wonderful little optical instrument. It is a one-power (1x), wide-angle telescope with its own portable mount. It is capable of seeing stars as faint as magnitude 6.5. It has a surface that gathers light, the *pupil*, and a lens that forms an image from the incoming light. This newly formed image is then projected onto the *retina* in the back of the eye (see FIG. 3-2).

The retina gives us two types of vision. Our ability to see detail, like the letters on this page, comes from the *cones* in the retina. The cones only work under bright light.

At night, we use another portion of the retina called the *rods*. Rods give us night vision. The retina contains many more rods than cones. When you sit in a room and turn off the overhead light, you will at first see nothing. Your eyes will gradually adjust to the darkness, called *dark adaptation*, and the rods become activated to the point where you can see. You can see in the dark because the rods are very sensitive to low

#1

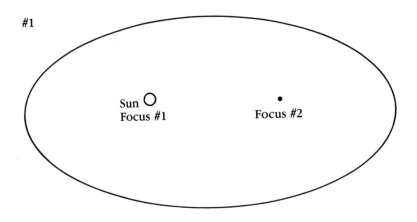

Sun ◯
Focus #1

Focus #2

#2

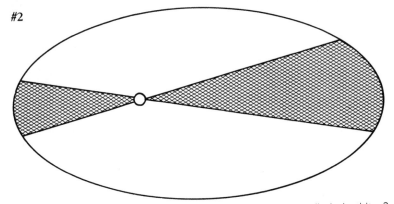

3-1 Kepler's Three Laws of Planetary Motion. 1. Planets travel in eliptical orbits. 2. A planet will sweep out equal areas of spaces in equal amounts. 3. The distance³ = period² (not shown).

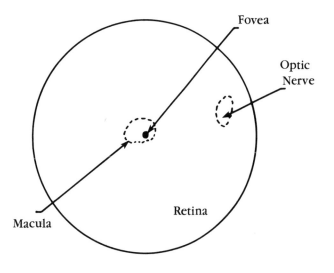

Fovea

Optic
Nerve

3-2 A cross section of the human eye.

Macula

Retina

light. Although they do not detect the fine detail that cones can, the rods do detect the differences in shading that allow us to distinguish very coarse detail.

The flashlight you carry outside to light up your charts or notebook might look small, but it can ruin your dark adaptation—even if the beam is small. When out observing, do not use any kind of white light; the best type to use is a red-filtered light. The red light will not affect your dark-adapted eyes. You can change the flashlight to project red light in several ways. If you can find a sheet of dark red, transparent plastic, cut a piece to fit over the flashlight lens. If you cannot find red plastic, remove the bulb and the reflector from the flashlight. Give the bulb a few coats of red nail polish and then replace the bulb only.

AIDING THE EYE

Observing the night sky with the unaided eye is a great way to get into the hobby of astronomy. Sooner or later, however, everyone gets a craving for a bit more.

Binoculars

The best instrument an observer can have is a good pair of binoculars (see FIG. 3-3). The lenses of binoculars gather more light than the unaided eye and they allow you to see fainter stars. Binoculars allow you to see the sky in its proper orientation, and they give it an almost three-dimensional look.

3-3 A pair of binoculars.

Binoculars are available in a wide variety of sizes. The size of binoculars is designated by two numbers separated by a times sign (7 × 35, 10 × 50, etc.). The first number refers to the magnification of the instrument. A 7 × 35 binocular magnifies the normal image seven times. A 10 × 50 pair magnifies the normal image ten times, etc. The second number is really the more important of the two; it refers to the size of the objective lens in the binoculars. A 7 × 35 pair has 35mm objective lenses, and a 10 × 50 pair has a 50mm objective lens. If the lenses are larger, the binoculars can gather more light and fainter objects can be seen.

An important thing to remember is: the larger the binocular objective, the heavier the instrument will be. This might not seem important now, but remember, you will have to hold the binoculars steady while you are observing. Each little tremor that runs through your body is going to be transmitted to the binoculars. The resulting view can be pretty bouncy!

A 7 × 50 pair of binoculars is about the largest instrument that can be hand-held. For bigger binoculars, make sure that you use a tripod—photo tripods are great. When you are using any size of binoculars, try to brace your arms against something—the arms of a chair, a fence, or a table all work well. If there is nothing around to lean against, try tucking your elbows into your sides to give yourself a more stable platform (see FIG. 3-4).

Telescopes

Many models of telescopes are available to the skywatcher, but they all work on the same principle: they all use an *objective* to form an image. Telescopes come in two basic types: the refractor and the reflector. The refractor uses a lens and the reflector uses a mirror (see FIG. 3-5).

The most important part of any telescope is its objective. The objective acts as an extension of the eye, but it gathers much more light than the eye can alone. The larger the objective of a telescope, is the fainter the stars that the telescope can see. The objective also plays an important role in the ability of the telescope to resolve detail, especially when you are viewing the Moon and planets.

When people hear the word *telescope*, the image of a *refractor* (FIG. 3-5) pops into mind. The refractor uses a lens as its objective. In 1609, Galileo used simple lenses to create his telescope. Today's refractors use the same principle to form their images.

Refractors are simple, but expensive instruments. In order for them to form images, light must pass completely through their objectives, so the lenses must be optically perfect. The slightest defect will cause the image to lose its sharpness. Because of this quality, the glass used to create the lens is very expensive.

Refractors can be very unwieldy instruments. Many refractors have long *focal lengths* (the distance it takes the objective to form an image), and have long tubes. They must also have large, high mountings so the observer can look through the eyepiece at the "working end."

The other type of telescope is the reflector (see FIG. 3-6). It uses a mir-

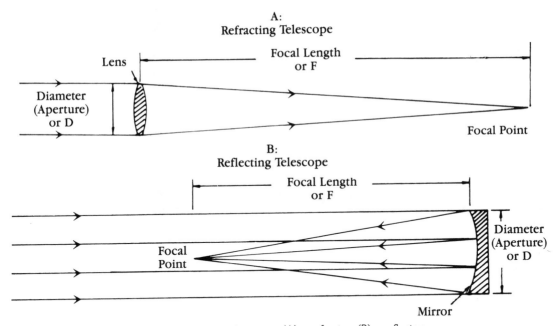

3-4 How light travels in telescopes: (A) a refractor, (B) a reflector.

ror to reflect the incoming light to form an image. The reflector was first designed by Sir Isaac Newton in 1666, and reflectors are still called *Newtonians*.

Reflectors are the "instrument of choice" for many observers. They are easy to construct and relatively inexpensive to purchase. Many amateurs have put in hours of labor grinding their own mirrors and been rewarded with an instrument that has served them well for years.

Clyde Tombaugh, the man who discovered the planet Pluto, is a good example. As a young man, he constructed a reflecting telescope. Recently, Tombaugh, now in his 80s, was approached by a major museum. Because he is the only living person who discovered a planet, the museum wanted to put together an exhibit that featured his telescope. When they asked him to donate it to the exhibit, he turned them down. "I'm still using it," was all he had to say!

There is one more type of telescope. The *Schmidt Cassegrain Telescope* (SCT) combines lenses and mirrors (see FIG. 3-7). SCTs have become very popular instruments since they were introduced in the 1970s. Their biggest advantage is portability. The short, compact tubes allow SCTs to be stored conveniently in trunklike lockers. They are easy to set up and are excellent for photography. SCTs are not as expensive as refractors, but not as inexpensive as reflectors.

PORTABLE SKIES

Whether you use your unaided eye, a pair of binoculars, or a telescope, you will need something to guide you through the night sky. Learning your way around the night sky is very much like planning a trip.

3-5 A refracting telescope.

When planning a trip, you must have an overall picture of where you want to go; for this you use a large-scale road atlas. Next, you might want to get a better idea of what awaits you at your destination. What nearby sites can you visit as you near your destination? For this, you can use a detailed state map. Finally, you will want an accurate street map of the area around your destination. It's the same way in the sky.

This book is your "large-scale road atlas." It will show you where the individual constellations are and how to find them on the dome of the sky. The charts in this book are simple; they show the constellations, their

3-6 A reflecting telescope.

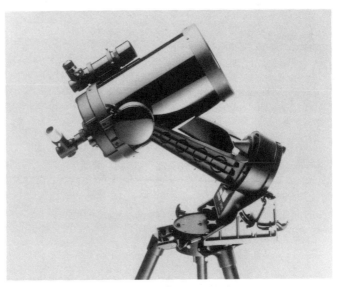

3-7 A Schmidt-Cassegrain telescope.

brightest stars, and some of the more interesting nearby sites. As an addition to this book, you can get a *planisphere* (FIG. 3-8), a device that will show what the sky will look like at any time on any day of the year. By using this book and a planisphere, you will receive a good background knowledge of the sky and the objects in it.

Much can be seen out there, so you might want to get more detailed charts. A wide variety of charts are available to the observer. A collection of charts is called a *star atlas*; many observers obtain *Norton's Star Atlas*. It contains charts covering the entire sky down to magnitude 6.5, the limit for the unaided eye, as well as valuable information on many deep-sky objects. This atlas also contains information on telescopes and observing techniques. Norton's has been in print since 1910, a record that shows how popular this book is with observers!

3-8A The planisphere can be your window to the stars. It shows the stars on any day of the year for any time of day.

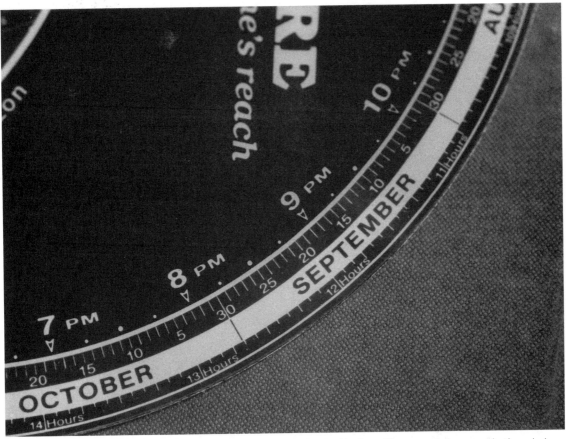

3-8B To use a planisphere, line up the time of day you want with the date. The stars that appear in the window reflect what the sky looks like at that time.

YOUR OBSERVING NOTEBOOK

Whether you observe the sky with the unaided eye, a pair of binoculars, or a telescope, it is important to record what you see. Observations are no good if you cannot remember what you have seen!

Keeping your observations in some kind of notebook or log is important. It can be a simple spiral-bound notebook or a blank book purchased at an art supply store. It can be anything as long as you use it to record your journey through the night sky.

Your notebook might start out small; the first observations might be nothing more than a listing of the stars you can see and the nightly sky conditions. As you progress as a skywatcher, your observations, comments, and notes will become more detailed. Your notebook will show not only what you see in the sky, but how you see the sky—through your eyes and observed in your individual way. Your notebook will become a source of joy and wonderment because you will be able to trace your development as an observer.

How you set up your observing notebook is up to you. After all, it is your observing notebook! You should record the date of each observing session and the time of each observation. What else you record and how you record it is your own way of dealing with the universe.

Chapter 4

Stars that never set

*C*ircling around the North Celestial Pole are six special constellations. Only two of them are very bright, but all are very well-known and important star figures. These stars are special because they are always above the northern horizon; they never set.

The constellations Ursa Minor, Draco, Camelopardalis, Cepheus, Cassiopeia, and most of Ursa Major are within a 42-degree circle of Polaris and the NCP (see FIG. 4-1). These six constellations are called the *circumpolar constellations*. They appear year round because they are the same distance from the NCP that it appears from the horizon. From Chicago, the NCP and Polaris are 42 degrees above the horizon. Any star that is within 42 degrees of the NCP will never drop below the horizon, so you can see it all year.

Although these constellations are visible any night of the year, how much you can see depends on where you live. Observers in the city see a slightly different sky than those in the country. With the growth of our cities, a problem has developed that few people think about: *light pollution*. This problem affects what we see in the night sky. The glare from hundreds of streetlights and buildings shine, not only on the streets, but into the sky. The light reflects off of tiny dust and moisture particles, creating a skyglow that makes it difficult or impossible to see faint stars. People observing under country skies are not faced with this problem, but their nearest city often appears as a glow on the horizon.

In the city, the circumpolar constellations that skim the northern horizon can be lost in the glow caused by shopping centers and streetlights. If you live in the country, you can easily see the circumpolar constellations throughout the year.

Light pollution does not only affect the circumpolar constellations. Each year, as the lights of our cities grow brighter, a little more of the sky is hidden from our view. Stars that once were blazing points of light now appear dimmer and harder to detect. Some objects, like the Andromeda

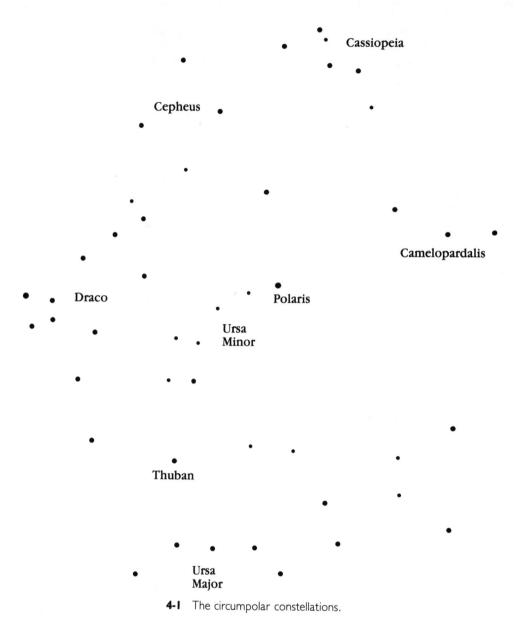

Cassiopeia

Cepheus

Camelopardalis

Draco

Polaris

Ursa
Minor

Thuban

Ursa
Major

4-1 The circumpolar constellations.

galaxy, get lost in the skyglow of the city lights even when the galaxy is high in the sky. The time will come when people, especially city dwellers, only will only be able to see the true beauty of the night sky through photographs or from the ceiling dome of a planetarium (see FIG. 4-2).

URSA MAJOR

Probably the best-known constellation in the sky is *Ursa Major*, the Great Bear. Ursa Major is marked by the asterism known as the Big Dipper. You can use this asterism to find your way around the sky.

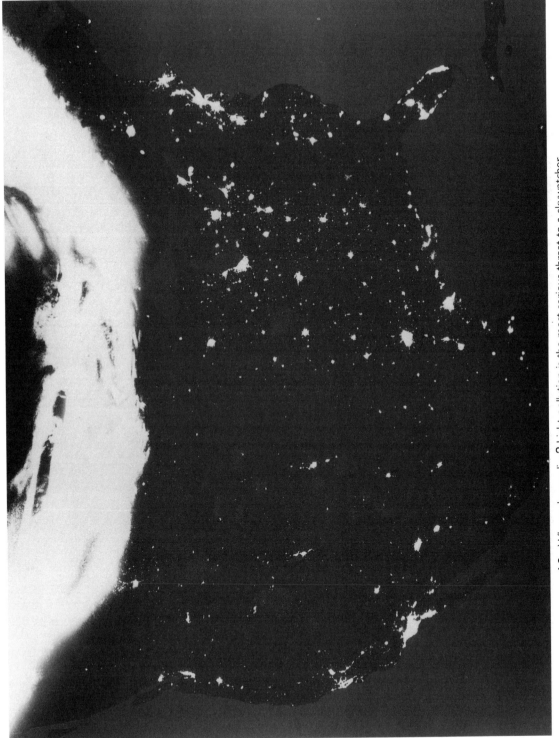

4-2 Where do you live? Light pollution is the most serious threat to a skywatcher.

Polaris and the Big Dipper

Using the two stars labeled as "pointers," Alpha (α) and Beta (β), you can easily find Polaris, the North Star. Just extend a line from the pointers for about 25 degrees, the span from the tip of your thumb to the tip of your little finger. Polaris is the brightest star in the constellation Ursa Minor, and it marks the North Celestial Pole. Extending a line between Gamma (γ) and Epsilon (ϵ) leads you to the "head" of Draco. A line from Gamma through Alpha will bring you to the faint collection of stars that make up Camelopardalis.

In addition to finding the other circumpolar constellations, you can use Ursa Major's asterism to find many of the constellations of the spring sky. Extending the arcing handle of the Dipper (following the "arc to Arcturus") makes it easy to locate the brightest star in Bootes. Extending this imaginary line farther ("driving a spike to Spica") brings you to *Spica*, the brightest star in the constellation of Virgo. By extending a line from Delta (δ) through Gamma (γ), you wind up at *Regulus*, the brightest star in Leo.

If you go outside at about 9:00 P.M. any night during February and March, you will see Ursa Major rising from the eastern horizon. At 9:00 P.M. during April and May, it is at its highest point in the sky; during these months, the Dipper can be found almost overhead. From June through August, the constellation slips from the evening sky toward the western horizon. The constellation is visible the rest of the year, from September through January at 9:00 P.M., but it is low on the northern horizon.

Mizar

The most interesting of the seven stars that make up the Big Dipper, Ursa Major's asterism, is located at the bend in the Dipper's handle. This star is called *Mizar*. In 1650, an Italian astronomer named Giovanni Riccioli used a simple refracting telescope to discover that Mizar was actually two stars. Mizar is a *Double Star*, two stars that revolve around a common center of gravity and travel through space together. His discovery caused quite a stir in the scientific community of the time.

Today, we know that double stars are common. Of the 200 billion stars that make up our galaxy, it is estimated that between 25 and 40 percent are double stars.

Double stars come in all shapes and sizes. Some of the stars that appear as doubles are the result of an optical illusion. Many stars are like Mizar, physically bound pairs of stars. However, some only fall together along our line of sight and appear as a pair, even though they are separated by hundreds of light-years. These are called *optical double stars* (FIG. 4-3). Another star, called *Alcor*, was once thought to make up a physical pair with the two stars of Mizar, but recent evidence seems to indicate that they are only an optical pair.

URSA MINOR

By following the pointer stars of the Big Dipper, you can find Polaris. In addition to being the star closest to the North Celestial Pole, Polaris is also

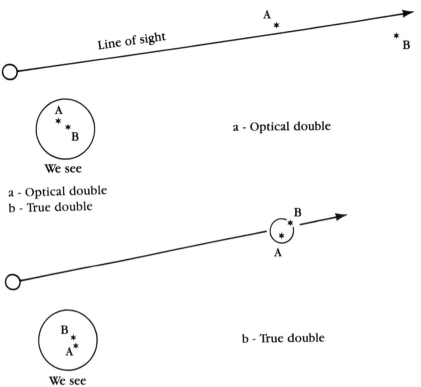

4-3 Double stars can be either (a) optical doubles or (b) physical binary stars.

the brightest star in the constellation *Ursa Minor*, the Lesser Bear. Ursa Minor is best seen during the latter part of June when it is on the meridian at 9:00 P.M. local time.

Like its "big brother," Ursa Major, Ursa Minor is easily identified by an asterism that looks like a dipper; so it is often called the "Little Dipper." The seven stars that make up this asterism, however, are much fainter and harder to find through the glare of city lights than the Big Dipper. Polaris marks the end of the Little Dipper's handle.

CAMELOPARDALIS

Camelopardalis, the Giraffe, is a collection of faint stars with a tongue-twister name! This constellation transits the meridian at 9:00 P.M. during early February, but its faint stars are rather hard to detect from the city. From a country location, you might be able to detect the small asterism of faint stars that forms a lop-sided kite next to Cassiopeia.

DRACO

Stretching between the two bears is the large constellation of *Draco*, the Dragon. The "head" of the dragon is marked by a box-shaped asterism. Draco is so large that different parts of its "body" transit at various times of the year. Its "tail" is on the meridian at 9:00 P.M. during May; part of its "body" during June and July; its "head" during August; and the "coils" of the dragon during September!

CASSIOPEIA

After Ursa Major, the easiest constellation to identify in the circumpolar sky is *Cassiopeia*, the Queen. Its distinctive "W"-shaped asterism is on the meridian at 9:00 P.M. during late November.

☆☆☆ Tycho's star

In 1572, Tycho Brahe, a Danish nobleman and astronomer, noticed a "new and unusual star, surpassing the other stars in brilliancy," shining almost overhead. This star brightened until it outshone Venus and was visible in full daylight!

The appearance of this "new and unusual" star was quite a shock to the astronomers of 1572. At that time, the stars and sky were considered fixed and unchanging. If that was true, what did this "new star" mean?

What Tycho saw that night was a truly rare event. He did not see a "new" star, but one of the four cases of a *supernova* that took place within our galaxy during historic times. Two other supernovae had occurred before Tycho saw his star: one appeared in A.D. 1006 and one in A.D. 1054. Another occurred in 1604 and was observed by the great astronomer, Johann Kepler. This supernova became known as *Kepler's Star*. Supernovae are the most violent events in the universe; they are the complete destruction of a star.

CEPHEUS

Nestled next to Cassiopeia is a group of stars that looks very much like a house. This asterism marks the constellation of *Cepheus*, the King. Cepheus is on the meridian at 9:00 P.M. during early October.

Delta Cephei: a yardstick in space

Located at the eastern corner of the base of the house is a star called Delta (δ) Cephei. Delta is a double star; one star is yellow and the other is blue. Delta is more than just a pretty double star, however; it is also a variable star. The brightness of Delta changes from magnitude 3.6 to magnitude 4.3 over a period of 5 days, 8 hours, 48 minutes.

The interesting thing about Delta is that its variability occurs with startling regularity. Many variable stars have little "glitches" in the time it takes them to reach their maximum or minimum brightness. However, Delta Cephei is so regular that you can set your watch to it! Its period is exactly 5 days, 8 hours, 48 minutes—never a minute longer or shorter.

Cepheid variables

Delta Cephei is not the only regularly variable star; many others exist. This type is called a *Cepheid* because Delta Cephei was the first regularly variable star to be found.

In 1912, Henrietta Leavitt of Harvard University discovered that this regularity was related to the amount of energy put out by the star—its *luminosity*. The more luminous a Cepheid variable is, the longer its period is. This relationship provided scientists with a way to determine distances on a galactic scale. If they could accurately measure the period of a Cepheid in a distant galaxy, they could determine the luminosity of the star. If they knew the luminosity of the star, they could determine the distance of the star and the galaxy it resides in by comparing how bright the star appears to its actual brightness. The Cepheids thus provided a means to measure intergalactic distances.

A PROJECT FOR THE YOUNG ASTRONOMER

Many amateur astronomers delight in locating faint objects thousands of light-years away, but how many can identify individual constellations? This search could be called a "long-range" project. Its objective is simple: identify and trace the outlines of as many of the 88 constellations as you can see from your observing location. The bright constellations with prominent asterisms, like Ursa Major, Cassiopeia, and Orion, will be easy to find. However, the fainter constellations, like Cancer, Vulpecula, and Pisces, will be challenging.

Chapter **5**

The brilliant sky of winter

*J*anuary and February bring cold weather and brilliant night skies. The stars visible on a winter evening are the brightest stars of the entire year. Dominating the sky are the bright constellations Taurus, Auriga, Orion, and Gemini (see FIG. 5-1). Throughout the winter months, these constellations are on or near the meridian, and well placed for viewing.

TAURUS

The first constellation to reach the meridian at 9:00 P.M. in the beginning of January is *Taurus*. Taurus is marked by the bright star, *Aldebaran*, and the prominent V-shaped asterism of stars, called the *Hyades* (FIG. 5-2).

Aldebaran shines at magnitude 0.8 and is the thirteenth brightest star in the sky. The first thing you notice about it is its color. Most people see it as reddish-orange. Astronomers once thought that the colors seen in the stars were an optical illusion. However, we now know that the color seen in Aldebaran and other stars can tell us much about the star itself.

January's night sky offers a very colorful display of stars. Aldebaran (reddish-orange) in Taurus, Capella (yellow) in Auriga; and Rigel (blue-white) and Betelgeuse (red) in Orion are all very bright and colorful stars. They also offer a look at the different kinds of stars that inhabit the night sky.

☆☆☆ Star color and star types

During the 1660s, Isaac Newton experimented with light and a prism (see FIG. 5-3). He discovered that the light we can see is made up of a rainbow of colors. At one end of the rainbow is violet and at the other is red.

In 1815, Joseph von Fraunhofer turned toward the Sun an instrument that would reveal the secrets of the stars. The instrument he used was a *spectroscope*, a simple device that allows a narrow

5-1 Orion and company.

beam of light to enter through a tiny slit. This light beam then goes through a prism, and the band of light is broken into component colors.

Looking closely at the resulting band of light, Fraunhofer noticed a number of tiny, dark lines. He painstakingly recorded the position of each of the 576 lines, but he didn't know what they meant. It would be 44 years before someone could decipher Fraunhofer's puzzle.

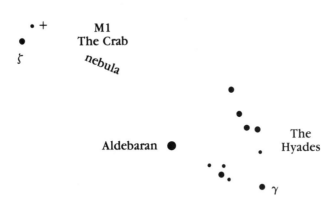

B

M45
The Pleiades

M1
The Crab

ξ

nebula

Aldebaran

The
Hyades

γ

5-2 Location of the Pleiades, the Hyades, and the Crab Nebula in Taurus.

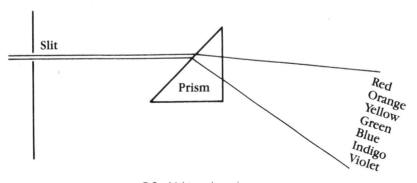

Slit

Prism

Red
Orange
Yellow
Green
Blue
Indigo
Violet

5-3 Light and a prism.

In 1859, two German scientists, Gustav Kirchoff and Robert W. Bunsen, realized that the lines Fraunhofer recorded were the "fingerprints" of the elements that made up the Sun! This technique was soon applied to the stars. Scientists discovered that they now had a tool to determine, not only the elements present in a star, but also the star's temperature.

In 1900, American astronomer Edward Pickering began to sort through the spectra of thousands of stars and found they fell into seven groups. He devised a series of letter codes, called spectral classes, to classify these groups. Spectral classes range from the hottest stars, *O*, to the coolest, *M*.

Astronomers soon found that the temperature of a star was also an indication of its age. Very hot stars are young and cooler stars are very old. They also found that star color is an indication of star temperature.

O stars are very young and hot, at 62,500 °F. The stars we see in the "Belt of Orion" are examples of blue-white O-type stars.

B stars are young and hot, at 35,500 °F. The blue-white star Rigel in Orion is a B-type star.

A stars burn at 17,500 °F. A-type stars are white like Sirius in Canis Major.

F stars burn at 12,100 °F. Procyon in Canis Minor is an example of the yellow-white F-type stars.

G stars, like the Sun, are middle-aged and burn at 10,300 °F. These stars are average and appear yellow. Capella in Auriga is another example of a G-type star.

K stars burn at 7,000 °F. Aldebaran, with its reddish-orange color, is a K-type star.

M stars are old and burn at only 4,000 °F. M-type stars are red, such as Betelgeuse in Orion.

In addition to these main classes of stars, additional classes cover the spectra of "peculiar" stars:

N stars are rich in carbon and deep red.

S stars are red and have unusual elements in their spectra.

The Hyades and Pleiades

Two striking objects in Taurus are easily visible to the unaided eye, even from the city. Aldebaran sits on the corner of the V-shaped asterism of stars called the *Hyades*. Slightly north and west of the Hyades is another collection of stars called the Pleiades (see FIG. 5-4). If you look closely at the Pleiades, you might notice that they resemble a dipper. In fact, they look so much like the dippers of the northern skies that this group is often misnamed the "Little Dipper." These groups of stars are more than random collections of suns; they are true *star clusters*.

Star clusters like the Hyades and Pleiades are called *open clusters*. Open clusters are groups of stars bound together by gravity. These stars appear scattered about, like paint flicked from a brush onto a wall. The open clusters are found in the spiral arms of our galaxy. Because these stars are located within the galaxy, they are sometimes called *galactic clusters*.

The Crab Nebula

In 1054, Chinese astronomers were startled by the appearance of a bright star where none had been seen before. This "guest star" was located near

5-4 The Pleiades star cluster.

one of the horns of Taurus. Today, a faint telescopic object is in the position recorded by these Chinese astronomers; this object is called the Crab Nebula (see FIG. 5-5). What the Chinese saw was one of the most violent events in the universe: the explosion of a *supernova*. What remains today are the whispy filaments of the explosion.

☆☆☆ The Messier catalog

In the 1700s, a French comet hunter named Charles Messier began to list objects that could be confused with comets. He assigned each of the objects he found a number. Messier listed his finds in the order that he observed them. The supernova remnant we call the Crab Nebula, discovered on September 12, 1758, became number 1 on his list. Messier's list was first published in 1774 and contained 45 objects. He expanded the list with supplements and later printings, until his final edition containing 103 objects was printed in 1781.

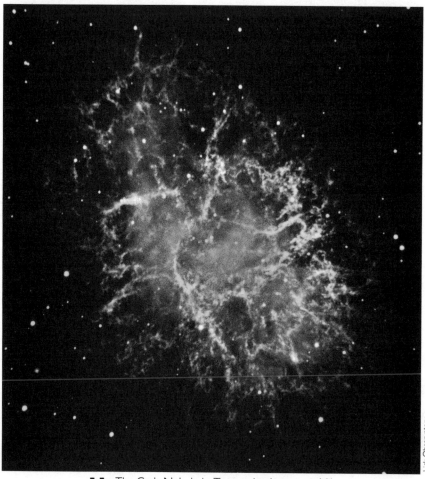

Lick Observatory

5-5 The Crab Nebula in Taurus also known as M1.

Astronomers have added to this list, and today the *Messier Catalog* contains 110 objects. The catalog contains the "best and the brightest" *deep-sky objects*. Each of these objects, preceded by the letter *M* (M1, M2, etc), is visible with either a pair of binoculars or a small telescope.

AURIGA

The constellation *Auriga* is easy to find in the January sky. Formed by a large house-shaped asterism, its first magnitude star, *Capella*, can be seen shining at the western corner of the "roof." Auriga is on the meridian at 9:00 P.M., during the middle of January.

Capella is a yellow star, like our Sun, and it is 45 light-years away. Capella is the closest first magnitude star to the present NCP, and it just misses being circumpolar for observers at 42 degrees north.

Epsilon Aurigae: the mystery star

Just south of Capella is a small triangle of stars called "the Kids." They are known by this curious name because the translation of *Capella* is "goat," and it is often called the "Goat Star." These three stars—Epsilon (ϵ), Zeta (ζ), and Eta (η)— are said to represent the Goat Star's "young."

A curious legend surrounds the star Epsilon. It was known to Arabic astronomers as the "He-Goat" until the star discovered the secret of youth and became a kid. This story seemed innocent enough, until the mid-1800s when it was discovered that Epsilon was a variable star.

A *variable star* does not shine with constant brightness. It brightens, fades, and then brightens again over a period of time, either because the star itself changes in some way or because another star blocks its light. Although some variable stars change their brightness over a period of hours, others can take hundreds of days to complete their cycle. Epsilon's brightness cycle is the longest of any of the 12,000 known variable stars: over 27 years.

Epsilon Aurigae is not a typical variable star. Since the confirmation of Epsilon's variability in 1847, many theories have been advanced to explain the star's fluctuations. It was determined in 1912 that the star's brightness changed because another object came between the Earth and the star, blocking its light. Stars like this are called *eclipsing binary stars*. However, astronomers could not find the object responsible for blocking out the main star's light. Epsilon seemed to have an invisible companion that should be visible in spite of the tremendous distance between us, 4,000 light-years. Scientists have calculated that the companion is huge. It would have to be large enough to block some of the light from the main star, which they determined to be 200,000 times brighter than our Sun.

Over the years since Epsilon was determined to be an eclipsing binary, many theories have been given as to why we cannot see the companion (see FIG. 5-6). One theory said that the companion was a star in the process of forming, and it periodically eclipsed the main star. Another theory created a large, flat disk of dust that blocked the light we see. Still another concept theorized that a black hole orbited the primary.

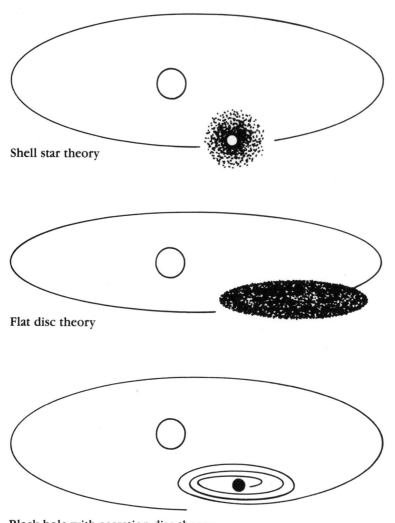

Shell star theory

Flat disc theory

Black hole with accretion disc theory

5-6 Epsilon Augigae and theories about why its light varies.

The current reigning theory shows the companion as a very hot star surrounded by a thick cloud of gas and dust. This theory explains why we cannot see the companion. If the cloud that surrounds the hot star is opaque, our instruments would not see the star at its center. Although this theory is presently accepted by many astronomers, Epsilon Aurigae has a long history of proving theories wrong. Only time will tell what the companion to Epsilon really is.

ORION

Orion is the "king" and the most easily recognized of all the constellations (see FIG. 5-7). The large asterism of four stars that forms the "body"

5-7 The constellation of Orion.

of the hunter and his three-star "belt" can be seen dominating the January sky. This constellation transits during the end of the month.

Orion stands astride the celestial equator with his upper "body" in the Northern Celestial Hemisphere and his lower "body" in the Southern Celestial Hemisphere. The celestial equator runs through his middle with the star Delta (δ) almost on the equator.

Orion is one of the few constellations that looks like its name. The arrangement of stars looks like a hunter. His head is marked by a small, triangular-shaped asterism of stars. In one hand, he holds his shield upraised to protect himself. In his other hand, he swings his mighty club and is ready to smash his celestial "enemy," Taurus the Bull.

Orion is easy to see under both city and country skies. Containing seven stars of the second magnitude or brighter, it cuts through all but the worst of the city skyglow.

On any clear winter night, you can see a soft glow shining from the tip of Orion's sword. Today, we know this glow as the *Great nebula* of Orion (see FIG. 5-8). Even though you can see this object, it was not mentioned in astronomy books before the invention of the telescope. Galileo never even turned his instrument on the glow.

It was not until 1611 that a relatively unknown astronomer named Nicholas Peiresc was credited for its discovery. For the next 45 years, this glow seemed to go unnoticed. In 1656, the astronomer and physicist, Christian Huygens, turned his telescope on the glow and published a drawing of the object. Messier listed the Great nebula as number 42 on his list of objects, after he observed it in March 1769.

☆☆☆ A stellar nursery

M42 is an excellent example of a *nebula*. *Nebulae* (the Latin plural for *nebula*) come in a variety of types. Some consist of gas and dust clouds that reflect the light of stars near them and are called *reflection nebula*. Others consist of thick dust clouds that cut off light from stars behind them and are named *dark nebula*. Still others are composed of gases that glow when they are exposed to radiation from nearby stars and are called *emission nebula*.

M42 is more than a simple emission nebula. Its glowing gases conceal something quite spectacular. Buried within the folds of gas and dust are *protostars*, stars that are just in the process of being born. Over untold millenia they have accumulated dust from the surrounding nebula; now the protostars are larger than our entire Solar System. Over time, these huge protostars will contract, shrinking smaller and exerting more pressure on their slowly building cores. In time, this tremendous amount of pressure will build to the point where the first fires of nuclear fusion will begin and the star will flare into life.

Orion offers astronomers a chance to see the entire range of stellar life. In M42, the Great nebula, stars are being born. In another area of the constellation are young stars, which scientists think have only recently begun to burn. Astronomers can study a star like Rigel to see what happens when a star burns its fuel faster than normal, and they can look at Betelgeuse to see what happens when a star becomes old and swollen with age.

GEMINI

Nestled just north and west of might Orion is *Gemini*. This constellation transits the meridian at 9:00 P.M. during the middle of February. Like Taurus, Gemini is one of the brighter constellations of the zodiac. Marked by the two bright stars *Castor* and *Pollux*, Gemini looks like two stick figures hanging in the sky.

5-8 The Great Nebula in Orion, a stellar nursery.

Among these "stick figures," William Herschel discovered Uranus in 1781. Scanning the skies for comets with a homebuilt 6.2-inch reflecting telescope, Herschel noticed a greenish disc near the star Eta (η) Geminorum. This disc was not a comet, but the seventh planet from the Sun, Uranus.

One hundred forty-nine years later, in 1930, Clyde Tombaugh was photographing star fields looking for an explanation to the wobbles in the orbits of Uranus and Neptune. On one of the photographic plates, he noticed a "star" that moved over the course of a few nights. It turned out to be the planet Pluto.

CANIS MAJOR

South and east of Orion is the constellation of *Canis Major*. Marked by *Sirius*, the brightest star in the sky, Canis Major can be found by simply extending a line through the belt of Orion to the southeast. Canis Major is on the meridian during the middle of February.

☆☆☆ Star brightness and luminosity

Shining at magnitude −1.4, Sirius is only exceeded in brightness by the Sun, Moon, Jupiter, Venus, and occasionally Mars.

Sirius appear so bright because it is a neighbor of the Sun. At a distance of 8.7 light-years, it is the closest bright star visible in the Northern Hemisphere.

Astronomers measure the brightness of stars in two ways. First, is the *apparent magnitude* of the star. This is how bright we see the star in the sky of Earth. The apparent brightness is measured on the scale devised by Hipparchus and discussed in chapter two.

The other way that the brightness of stars and other objects is measured, is by the *absolute magnitude*. To measure the absolute magnitude of a star, astronomers "take a page" from the old theories of the Universe and imagine that all the stars are 32.5 light-years from Earth. If the Sun were moved to a point 32.5 light-years from us, it would no longer appear as a magnitude −26 object, but as an average-looking star of magnitude 4.8! So, the absolute magnitude of the Sun is 4.8. If Sirius was 32.5 light-years from us, it would appear as a magnitude 1.4 star—still bright, but not the dazzler we see in the winter sky.

The absolute magnitude of a star gives us an indication of its luminosity. Rigel, for example, shines as a magnitude 0.14 star, but it is at a distance of 900 light-years. Rigel puts out a tremendous amount of energy to be that far away and still appear so bright. If Rigel was moved to 32.5 light-years from the Sun, it would shine at an absolute magnitude of −7.1!

Sirius and the Pup

Sirius held a surprise for scientists. In 1862, the telescope-making firm of Alvan Clark & Sons of Massachusetts was completing work on what was then the largest telescope in the world, an 18.5-inch refractor. While testing the accuracy of the instrument, Alvan Clark decided to observe Sirius. Its brightness would reveal any flaws in the telescope's lens. Clark was surprised to see a faint star near the almost overpowering glare of Sirius. He had discovered a companion to the "Dog Star," and it was dubbed the "Pup" (see FIG. 5-9).

Lick Observatory

5-9 Sirius and its small companion. The "spikes" around brighter Sirius are created by a special mask to allow us to see the "Pup."

However, the Pup is more than just another component of a double-star system. The Pup, or Sirius-*B* (its scientific name), is a *white-dwarf star*. A white dwarf is an extremely small, but massive star. In the case of the Pup, it has almost the same amount of *mass* (the matter that makes up the object) as our sun, but it is only about 5 times the size of the Earth. A tiny bit of matter from the Pup would weigh an immense amount. If you could fill a matchbox with the matter from the Pup, the box would weigh over 1¼ tons!

CANIS MINOR

Directly east of Betelgeuse in Orion is the bright star *Procyon*. It marks the constellation of *Canis Minor*. Canis Minor is on the meridian during the last week of February.

ERIDANUS

Stretching west from Orion is the constellation *Eridanus*. Although it is almost twice the size of its neighbor, Orion, Eridanus is composed of stars considerably more faint. Eridanus is so large that it begins its transit from the meridian in early December, but not until January 24 does the last of its stars, Beta (just Northwest of Rigel), begin its journey toward the western horizon.

Eridanus is also the first constellation that observers from the midlatitudes encounter that extends below the southern horizon. As far as stargazing from the United States is concerned, the brightest star in the constellation, *Archernar*, is only visible to observers in southern Texas and Florida. Achernar, the ninth brightest star in the sky, is located only 32.5 degrees from the Southern Celestial Pole.

The most interesting star in this constellation is a third-magnitude star labeled *Epsilon Eridani*. It doesn't look like much compared to the brilliant stars of nearby Orion, but looks can be deceiving. In addition to being one of the nearest stars to the Sun (10.8 light-years away), only Alpha Centauri and Sirius are closer.

Astronomers have detected an unseen companion circling the star. Unlike the invisible companion of Epsilon Aurigae, the reason we cannot see the companion of Epsilon Eridani is understood. Orbiting at a distance of 716 million miles from this K-type star is what scientists believe to be a planet similar to Jupiter, but much larger.

LEPUS

Nestled under the "feet" of Orion is the small constellation *Lepus*. Lepus is another constellation that tends to get lost among the brilliant stars of its neighbor, Orion. You can find Lepus by looking for a small asterism shaped like a lopsided box directly below Orion. Lepus transits the meridian during the last week of January.

MONOCEROS

Between Canis Major on the south, Canis Minor on the north, and Orion on the west is the faint constellation of *Monoceros*. Monoceros is on the meridian at 9:00 P.M. during the last half of February.

PUPPIS

South of Canis Major and skimming the southern horizon is the constellation *Puppis*. At one time, Puppis was part of a huge constellation called *Argo Navis*. In 1930, however, the constellation was broken up into "manageable" pieces that include Puppis and 3 other constellations. Puppis is on the meridian, low in the south, at 9:00 P.M. during late February.

COLUMBA

Located just below Lepus is the small constellation of *Columba*. Created by the starmapper Bayer in 1603, Columba is made up of two third magnitude stars and several fainter ones. It crosses the meridian at 9:00 P.M. in early February.

CAELUM

Next to Columba and extending below the southern horizon is the constellation *Caelum*. In 1752, the starmapper Nicolas LaCaille created many of the constellations seen in the southern skies. When he created them, he felt that they should represent tools used by artists and scientists. Caelum represents the chisel used by sculptors and engravers.

A PROJECT FOR THE YOUNG ASTRONOMER

The stars of the winter sky are not only bright, but colorful. The purpose of this project is to see which stars show definite color. Like many of the other projects in this book, this project can extend over the entire year.

Many of the brighter stars show color, but do fainter stars also show color? You can work on this project with the unaided eye and/or a pair of binoculars.

The following table of color types (TABLE 5-1) has been adapted from a number of sources. It is primarily keyed to the spectral colors shown by stars.

Table 5-1

Rating	Color	Spectral type
1	Blue	O
2	Blue-white	B
3	White	A
4	Yellow-white	F
5	Yellow	G
6	Orange	K
7	Red	M

Observe the bright stars and determine the color of each using this table. Observe fainter stars and see if they exhibit any color. When observing your "target" star, try looking at it through a short tube; a paper towel tube is perfect. The tube will ever so slightly eliminate stray light and heighten the star's color.

Record your observations in your notebook. Note the date, time, and weather conditions, and pay particular attention to the height of your target above the horizon. Is there any difference in the star color as it moves higher or lower in the sky?

Chapter **6**

Harbingers of spring

With the brilliant constellations of winter moving toward the western horizon, another set of star figures moves toward the meridian. The stars of March, April, and May seem rather dull compared to their winter brothers, but they are no less interesting (see FIG. 6-1).

LYNX

The first constellation to reach the meridian during March is the long, rambling line of faint stars that makes up *Lynx*, the Lynx. During the first week of March, Lynx is almost overhead at 9:00 P.M.

Located in Lynx is a faint telescopic object called *NGC 2419*. The NGC (New General Catalog) is a listing of 13,000 deep-sky objects. A *deep-sky object* is any object that is found outside our Solar System, including both open and globular star clusters, nebulae, and galaxies.

NGC 2419 is a globular cluster. What makes this faint, eleventh-magnitude object interesting is the fact that it is the most distant globular cluster in the Milky Way. It was discovered in 1788 by the great astronomer Sir William Herschel.

In 1922, Harlow Shapely of Mt. Wilson Observatory calculated that NGC 2419 was 182,000 light-years from the Sun and 210,000 light-years from the center of our galaxy. He dubbed the cluster the "Intergalactic Wanderer" because of the over 100 globular clusters discovered it is the most distant from the Earth.

CANCER

Directly south of Lynx is the constellation *Cancer*, the Crab. Cancer is a rather faint constellation and it reaches the meridian at 9:00 P.M. during the middle of March. Cancer is a member of the *zodiac*, a group of twelve

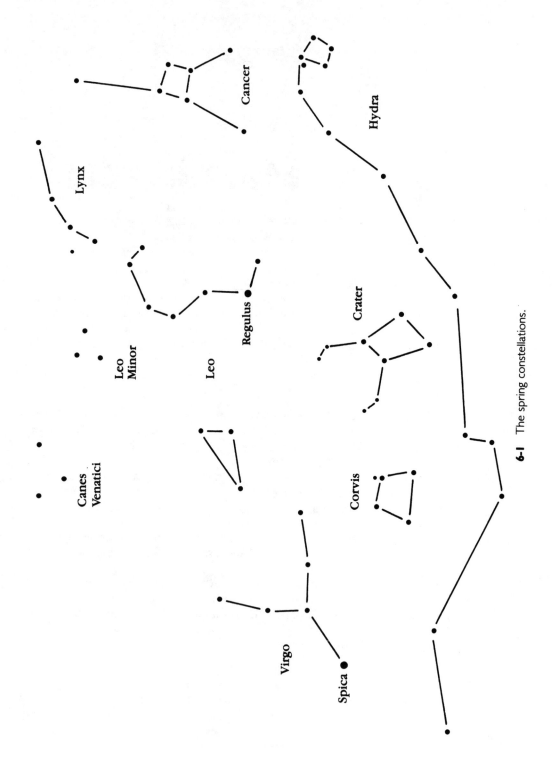

6-1 The spring constellations.

Cancer

Hydra

Lynx

Leo
Minor

Leo

Regulus

Crater

Canes
Venatici

Corvis

Virgo

Spica

constellations that lie along the path, called the *ecliptic*, that the sun, follows across the sky. In addition to Cancer, the zodiac includes Taurus, Gemini, Leo, Virgo, Libra, Scorpius, Sagittarius, Capricornus, Aquarius, Pisces, and Aries.

The Beehive cluster

Cancer is home to a large open cluster called the *Beehive cluster* (see FIG. 6-2). This cluster bears a number of names, including the *Praesepe cluster*. It is also the 44th object of Messier's list (M44) and NGC 2632.

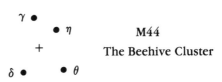

6-2   The location of the Beehive star cluster.

Integrated magnitude

Under clear skies, the Beehive is visible to the unaided eye. It is listed in catalogs as being magnitude 3.1, but this magnitude can be deceiving. The magnitudes for many deep-sky objects are listed at their *integrated magnitudes*. This magnitude is what the object would be if all the stars in it were concentrated into one spot in the sky. The Beehive, however, is a very large object. It covers over one full degree of the sky—two full-moon diameters. At this size, its light is spread rather thinly, making the Beehive rather difficult to see under all but the darkest sky conditions.

HYDRA

Beginning south of Cancer and stretching off to the east is the largest con-stellation in the sky, *Hydra*, the Sea Serpent. You can find the "head" of Hydra, a small boxlike asterism below Cancer, but it can be a challenge to trace the entire length of the sea monster's body as it winds toward the east.

Hydra's head reaches the meridian at 9:00 P.M. during the middle of March. The middle of its "body" reaches the meridian a month later, dur-ing the middle of April. The end of Hydra's "tail" does not reach the meridian until mid-May!

LEO

The brightest of the constellations in the spring sky is *Leo*, the Lion. An easy-to-find asterism that looks like a backward question mark denotes the head and shoulders of the lion. A fainter asterism, which looks like a triangle, marks the hind quarters and tail of the celestial beast. Leo transits the meridian during the middle of April at 9:00 P.M..

Leo is marked by the bright star, *Regulus*. At magnitude 1.33, Regulus is the twenty-first brightest star in the sky. Regulus is a *B*-type star, so it has a blue-white color. Some 85 light-years from the Sun, Regulus is a very luminous star. Its absolute magnitude is −0-7, and it puts out 160 times more energy than the Sun.

LEO MINOR

Above Leo is the small, faint constellation of *Leo Minor*, the Little Lion. On the meridian early in April, it contains a triangle-shaped asterism made up of rather faint stars.

SEXTANS

Between Leo and Hydra is the small, dim constellation of *Sextans*, the Sextant. Sextans reaches the meridian at 9:00 P.M. during late April.

CANES VENATICI

High on the meridian during mid-May is the small constellation of *Canes Venatici*, the Hunting Dogs. This constellation is marked by two stars, Alpha and Beta. Both stars are fairly dim for city observers, so you might have to hunt for them.

COMA BERNICES

Directly south of Canes Venatici is the constellation *Coma Bernices*, Bernice's Hair. Coma is a rather strange-looking constellation. On the star maps, it is hard to pick out an identifying asterism, but three rather faint stars form a large right triangle.

VIRGO

As May slips away, you will see a bright star moving toward the meridian in the south. This is *Spica*, the brightest star in *Virgo*, the Virgin. Virgo is a large constellation; the area around Spica reaches the meridian at 9:00 P.M. in late May. Virgo is marked by a bowl-shaped asterism west of Spica, and the bright star forms a "handle."

Spica is the fifteenth brightest star in the sky. It is a *B*-type star that shines at magnitude 0.9 and is 80 light-years away. Like many *B* stars, Spica is very luminous, some 2,300 times more than the Sun.

☆☆☆ A cloud of galaxies

The area on the Virgo-Coma Bernices border does not look like much to the unaided eye. However, if you turn even a small telescope on the area, you will see the galaxies spread like stars across the field of view. This area is called the *Virgo Galaxy Cluster* (see FIG. 6-3). Over 3000 galaxies can be seen in this cluster in photos taken with large telescopes. Of these, 100 can be seen with telescopes as small as 8 inches in diameter.

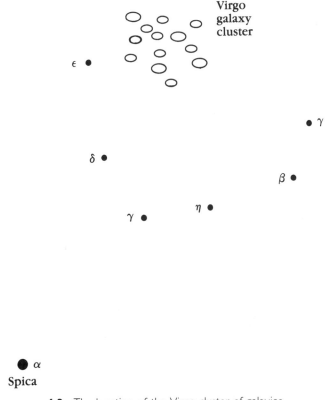

6-3 The location of the Virgo cluster of galaxies.

The Virgo Cluster is one of the nearest groups of galaxies to the Milky Way. It is about 42 million light-years from us. Many types of galaxies form the Virgo cluster.

Galaxies come in a wide variety of shapes, but fall into three major categories: spirals, ellipticals, and irregulars.

Our Milky Way is a *spiral galaxy*, as are many of the galaxies in the Virgo Cluster. Spiral galaxies consist of a central nucleus surrounded by a disk that stretches out into spiral arms (FIG. 6-4). Spiral

6-4 Two typical spiral galaxies (A) M31 in Andromeda,

Lick Observatory

galaxies contain both young and old stars. The young stars are located in the spiral arms and the older stars are in the central nucleus. Around the spirals is a halo of globular clusters. This halo extends around the nucleus of the galaxy. Most of the bright galaxies that can be seen through our telescopes are spirals.

We see these galaxies in a number of orientations. Some are seen almost edge on, and the vast lanes of dust that make up part of

6-4 (B) M81 in Ursa Major.

the spiral arms are visible. Other spiral galaxies can be seen almost face on and look very much like a pinwheel. Between these two views are almost limitless variations showing all sides of the distant galaxies.

Another type of galaxy is called an *elliptical galaxy* (see FIG. 6-5). Ellipticals look like the nucleus of spiral galaxies, but they have no apparent spiral arm structures. Ellipticals are composed of older stars.

6-5 M87 in Virgo, a typical elliptical galaxy.

The last major type of galaxy is the *irregular galaxy* (FIG. 6-6). These galaxies have no apparent structure and almost appear to be cosmic afterthoughts. Irregular galaxies can also look as if they have undergone huge cosmic catastrophes—like they have been ripped apart by some gigantic explosion. The Large and Small Magellanic Clouds, visible in the southern skies, are examples of irregular galaxies.

CRATER

Perched on the back of Hydra and below the tail of Leo is the constellation *Crater*, the Cup. Its cup- or bowl-shaped asterism is on the meridian at 9:00 P.M. during the middle of May.

CORVUS

South of the bowl of Virgo and next to Crater is a small group of stars shaped like a trapezoid. This is the small constellation of *Corvus*, the

6-6 The Large Magellanic Cloud is a typical irregular galaxy.

Lick Observatory

Crow. Like Crater, it also seems to be perched on the back of Hydra. Corvus transits the meridian at 9:00 P.M. during the last week of May.

PYXIS

Below Hydra is the faint constellation of *Pyxis*, the Ship's (Argo Navis) Compass. Made up of third- and fourth-magnitude stars, the constellation reaches the meridian at 9:00 P.M. during early April.

ANTLIA

Also located below Hydra, but next to Pyxis, is the constellation of *Antlia*, the Air Pump. Although larger than Pyxis, Antlia is also faint. It reaches the meridian at 9:00 P.M. during late April and early May.

CENTAURUS

Low on the southern horizon during late May and early June is the large constellation *Centaurus*, the Centaur. Unfortunately for most observers in the United States, Centaurus is only partially visible. Its brightest stars remain below the horizon for most observers.

Centaurus holds the Sun's nearest neighbor in space. *Alpha Centauri* is 4.3 light-years away, a mere "stone's throw" in the vast reaches of space.

A PROJECT FOR THE YOUNG ASTRONOMER

The biggest problem facing the astronomer, whether amateur or professional, is light pollution. Light spilling into the sky from fixtures in backyards and shopping centers is stealing the stars. This project will help you determine just how bad light pollution is at your observation site.

During the Spring, Leo is prominent and contains stars such as first-magnitude Regulus to fifth-magnitude Kappa (see FIG. 6-7). Begin by determining the faintest star you can see when the constellation is at the

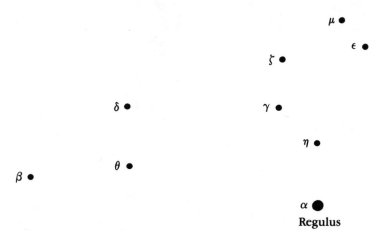

6-7 The stars in Leo can be used to estimate the clarity of the sky. Magnitudes are: Alpha (1), Beta (2), Gamma (2), Delta (2.5), Epsilon (3), Eta (3.5), and Mu (4).

meridian. Then determine the faintest you can observe when the constellation is near the eastern horizon (rising) and the western horizon (setting).

Normally, the constellation will lose a certain number of magnitudes when it is near the horizon because you are looking through more of the Earth's atmosphere. Theoretically, if you can see stars as faint as fourth-magnitude near zenith, normal *atmospheric extinction* will cause you to lose 1 magnitude for stars 10 degrees above the horizon and another 0.5 magnitude for stars 20 degrees above the horizon. So you should be able to see third-magnitude stars when they are 10 degrees above the horizon and 2.5-magnitude stars when they are 20 degrees up. Compare your observations of Leo. Are you within these theoretical limits? Whatever else is lost is probably because of light pollution.

Chapter 7

Keystones and Scorpions

*J*une, July, and August bring mild evenings, a beautiful sky, and later sunsets. These months also bring a mixed bag of constellations to the meridian. Some are bright and others are faint, but they are all very distinctive and easy to identify (see FIG. 7-1).

The Milky Way is prominent directly to the south in the constellation Scorpius and runs through Serpens and Ophiuchus.

BOOTES

Riding high in the sky during late June is the constellation of *Bootes*, the Herdsman. Marked by the bright star, *Arcturus*, Bootes is recognized by a kite-shaped asterism with Arcturus in the "tail" of the kite.

☆☆☆ Hertzsprung-Russell Diagrams

In the early 1900s, scientists were puzzled by the information that stellar spectra were revealing. How could a star like Arcturus, for example, appear so bright if its spectra showed it to be a relatively cool star? In 1905, the Danish astronomer Ejnar Hertzsprung suggested that the only way for a relatively cool star to appear bright was because of its tremendous size.

A star will output a certain amount of energy over its surface area. A cool star, like Arcturus, does not output much energy per square mile of its surface area. However, it will appear bright if that low output of energy is spread over a great surface area. For Arcturus to appear as bright as it does (100 times more luminous than the Sun), it would have to be 23 times larger than the Sun!

While Hertzsprung was considering this problem of giant stars, another astronomer, Henry Russell, was doing similar work. In 1913, he began to plot stars on a graph. Along the vertical axis, he listed absolute magnitudes, and along the horizontal axis, he listed

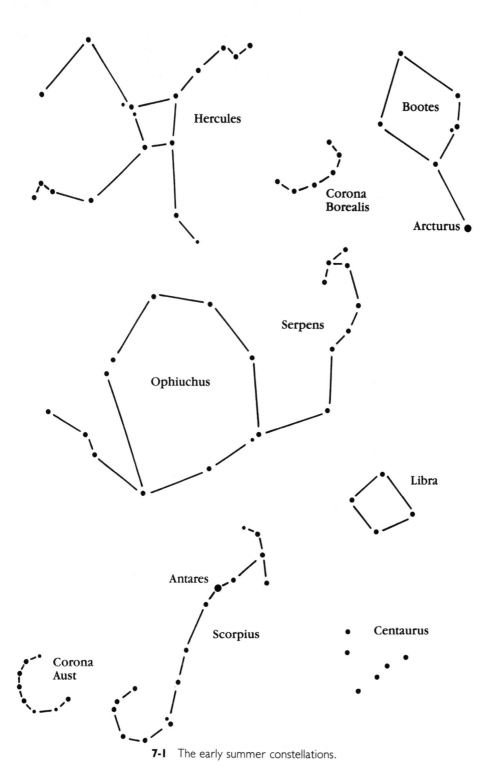

7-1 The early summer constellations.

spectral classes (see FIG. 7-2). Although he didn't know it at the time, Hertzsprung had worked out a similar graph that today is called the *Hertzsprung-Russell Diagram*, or the *H-R Diagram*.

When they first started plotting stars on their graphs, Hertzsprung and Russell both expected to find a random distribution of star types. However, the resulting diagrams showed that stars tended to cluster. A large, curving band, the *main sequence*, ran diagonally across the diagram. Main-sequence stars comprise 90 percent of all stars.

The position of a star on the main sequence is determined by its mass. Stars more massive, and therefore more luminous, than our Sun are located toward the upper left of the main sequence. Stars like our Sun are clustered toward the center of the main-sequence band. Stars less massive and luminous than the Sun are at the lower right of the diagram. Above the main sequence, to the upper right, are giant and supergiant stars. Below and to the left are massive white-dwarf stars.

CORONA BOREALIS

Just east of Bootes is an easily recognized semicircle of stars that marks the constellation of *Corona Borealis*, the Northern Crown. During mid-July, Corona reaches the meridian at 9:00 P.M.

HERCULES

High overhead during July and August is a large constellation marked by four stars that create a keystone-shaped asterism. This is the hero, *Hercules*. The keystone marks the body of Hercules, with his arms and legs stretching off around it.

M13: The Great Cluster

To the unaided eye, the most famous feature in the Hercules constellation appears as a faint, fuzzy blob of light between the western two stars on the keystone (see FIG. 7-3). This "faint fuzzy" is number 13 on Charles Messier's list. M13 is a *globular star cluster*, and it is probably the best example of this type of deep-sky object.

Globular clusters are tightly packed, spherical groups of stars. Where open clusters might contain dozens or even hundreds of stars, globulars contain hundreds of thousands of stars. Some larger globulars, like M13, might contain over 1 million stars!

Another difference between open and globular clusters is their location. With few exceptions, open clusters are found within the spiral arms of the galaxy. Globular clusters are mostly found in the halo that surrounds our galaxy.

The stars that make up globulars are also different from those in open clusters. The stars of the open clusters are mostly young, hot stars, called *Population I* stars. Globulars, on the other hand, consist of much older stars like red giants and white dwarfs, called *Population II* stars (FIG. 7-4).

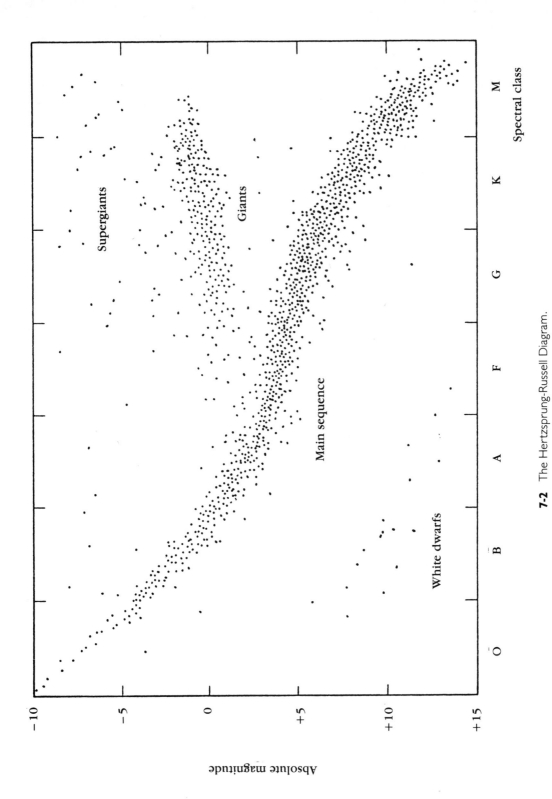

7-2 The Hertzsprung-Russell Diagram.

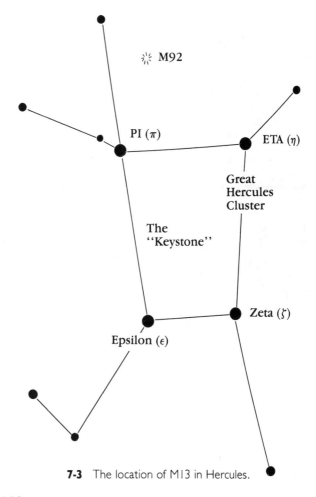

M92

PI (π)

ETA (η)

Great
Hercules
Cluster

The
"Keystone"

Zeta (ζ)

Epsilon (ε)

7-3 The location of M13 in Hercules.

SCORPIUS

Located in the southern sky, *Scorpius* is one of the few constellations that looks like its namesake. You can easily see the shape of a giant scorpion with its stinger brushing the horizon. The middle of this giant beast, marked by the red star *Antares*, crosses the meridian at 9:00 P.M. during the last week of July.

At the "heart" of the scorpion is the red star Antares. Antares is the sixteenth brightest star in the sky and it shines at magnitude 0.9. Because of its red color, Antares is often called the "Rival of Mars."

CORONA AUSTRALIS

Just to the east of the Scorpion's tail is the small constellation *Corona Australis*, the Southern Crown. For most of the United States, this constellation lies very low on the southern horizon. Made up of fourth- and fifth-magnitude stars, it is hard to pick out. The Southern Crown is highest above the horizon late in August, when it transits the meridian at 9:00 P.M.

7-4 Also located in Hercules is the globular cluster M92.

LIBRA

Located west of Scorpius is a box-shaped asterism that marks the zodiacal constellation of *Libra*, the Scale. The stars of Libra are only third- and fourth-magnitude, making it a difficult constellation to find. Libra is even tougher to locate because it is best seen low in the south during the first week of July at 9:00 P.M. The haze of warm summer evenings makes stars that are low in the south even harder to find.

LUPUS

Just skimming the southern horizon west of Scorpius and south of Libra is the constellation *Lupus*, the Wolf. Look for this constellation during the middle of July.

SERPENS AND OPHIUCHUS

Stretching east of Bootes, south of Hercules, and north of Scorpius are the constellations *Serpens*, the Snake, and *Ophiuchus*, the Snakebearer. These constellations are so intertwined that it is difficult to see where one ends and the other begins.

Serpens has been divided into two sections separated by Ophiuchus (see FIG. 7-5). West of Ophiuchus is *Serpens Caput*, the "Head of the Serpent." East of Ophiuchus is *Serpens Cauda*, the "Body of the Serpent." The "head" of the serpent crosses the meridian at 9:00 P.M. during mid-July, and the "body" transits during late August. Ophiuchus crosses the meridian during early August.

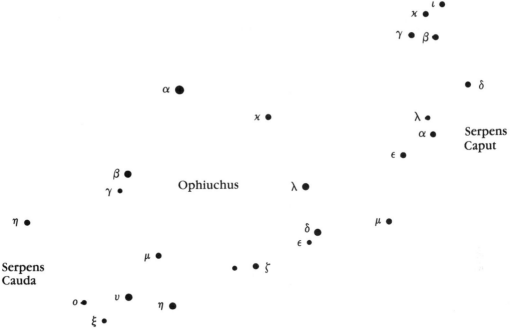

7-5 The "intertwined" constellations of Ophiuchus and Serpens.

As stated earlier, the ecliptic marks the path of the Sun across the sky, and all constellations of the zodiac lie along this imaginary line. In all, there are 12 zodiacal constellations, but there should be 13! Maybe the ancient astronomers and astrologers felt that thirteen was an unlucky number, so they left the zodiac at twelve.

Ophiuchus should be included in the zodiac because the ecliptic passes right through the constellation. In fact, the Sun spends more time in Ophiuchus than in neighboring Scorpius! So, if you were born between November 21 and December 16, your sign is actually Ophiuchus, the Snakebearer!

A PROJECT FOR THE YOUNG ASTRONOMER

By my count, 33 of the objects in the Messier catalog are magnitude 6.5 or brighter. How many of these can you see with no optical aid?

You can spread this project over a number of months because the targets are fairly well spread across the sky. Eleven of these are in the winter sky, four in the spring, thirteen in the summer, and five in the autumn (see TABLE 7-1).

Record each of your observations in your notebook. List the date, time, sky conditions, and a brief description of what each object looks like. If you like, make a sketch of the object against the background stars. Take your time; this project has no time limit.

Table 7-1 A Seasonal List of Messier Objects That Can Be Seen with the Naked Eye.

M#	Constellation	Type	Mag.
	Winter Targets		
45	Taurus	OC	1.2
36	Auriga	OC	6.0
37	Auriga	OC	5.6
38	Auriga	OC	6.4
42	Orion	EN	4.0
35	Gemini	OC	5.1
41	Canis Major	OC	4.5
50	Monoceros	OC	5.9
46	Puppis	OC	6.1
47	Puppis	OC	4.4
93	Puppis	OC	6.2
	Spring Targets		
48	Hydra	OC	5.8
44	Cancer	OC	3.1
3	Canes Venatici	GC	6.4
5	Serpens	GC	5.8
	Summer Targets		
13	Hercules	GC	5.9
92	Hercules	GC	6.5
4	Scorpius	GC	5.9
6	Scorpius	OC	4.2
7	Scorpius	OC	3.3
16	Serpens	EN + OC	6.0
8	Sagittarius	EN	5.8
21	Sagittarius	OC	5.9
22	Sagittarius	GC	5.1
23	Sagittarius	OC	5.5
25	Sagittarius	OC	4.6
11	Scutum	OC	5.8
39	Cygnus	OC	4.6
	Autumn Targets		
2	Aquarius	GC	6.5
15	Pegasus	GC	6.4
31	Andromeda	G	3.4
33	Triangulum	G	5.7
34	Perseus	OC	5.2

Chapter 8

Around the summer triangle

August and September bring more warm nights and bright stars, making it relaxing to go out under the stars. The summer constellations offer us a look at many wonders of the universe.

A prominent ''super''-asterism sits overhead during these evenings. If you draw a line from Vega east to Deneb, then south to Altair, and then back north to Vega, you have created the *Summer Triangle* (see FIG. 8-1). This asterism is not made up of the stars of one constellation, but rather of three constellations.

Also prominent in the late summer sky is the Milky Way. It runs across the sky from the circumpolar constellation of Cassiopeia, low in the northeast, through Cygnus, almost overhead, to Scorpius, low in the southwest.

LYRA

On the meridian at 9:00 P.M. at the end of August is a small parallelogram-shaped asterism that forms *Lyra*. This constellation represents an ancient musical instrument called a *lyre*, something akin to a harp. The constellation seems to hang from the bright star *Vega*, which is sometimes called the ''Harp Star.'' Vega is the brightest of the three stars that form the Summer Triangle.

Vega: the birth of a solar system

Shining at magnitude 0.04, Vega is the fifth brightest star in the sky. It is a relatively close neighbor of the Sun, only 27 light-years away. In fact, some scientists believe that our solar system is traveling toward Vega's area of space at a speed of 12 miles per second. However, even if we were aimed directly at Vega, it would take over 450,000 years to cover the distance at that speed.

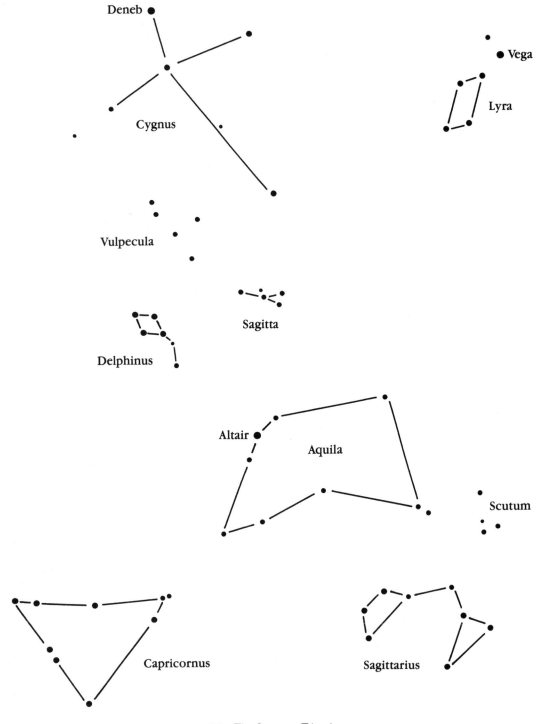

8-1 The Summer Triangle.

Vega is a very luminous, hot star. It is burning at about twice the temperature of the Sun, and it produces 58 times more energy than the Sun. Vega is about 2.7 million miles in diameter.

Astronomers once thought that Vega was a variable star because observations made during 1918 and 1935 seemed to indicate that it changed in brightness. The brightness change was so slight that complex instruments were needed to detect the changes. By the 1960s, it was decided that this "variability" was not caused by Vega, but by slight changes in a nearby star that astronomers used as a comparison for Vega.

The age of astronomical spacecraft might give a more interesting answer to the possible variability of Vega. Recent observations seem to indicate that Vega is surrounded by a cloud of material that might be the beginning of the formation of a solar system! Scientists believe that this material is like the asteroid belt found in our solar system. Eventually, the material in this cloud could combine to create planets.

If a cloud of debris is around a newly forming Vegan system of planets, it could explain why the light from that star varies. As we look into the system, the dust and debris moving around Vega could block out some of the light headed our way, causing the outcoming light to vary.

The Ring nebula: the death of a star

Although a young solar (or Vegan) system might be forming at one end of Lyra, a classic example of a dead star is at the other end of the constellation.

When an average star, like the Sun, gets old, it begins to change. As the star uses up its nuclear fuel—hydrogen—it creates helium ash. This ash builds up in the core of the star, and eventually the star begins to cool and swell. When the star reaches a certain size, it will blow off its outer layer of matter. This matter will float off into space, expanding and forming a shell. It is this shell that we see as the *Ring nebula* (see FIG. 8-2).

Discovered in 1779 by the French astronomer Antoine Darquier, the Ring nebula was described as looking "like a faded planet," so it became known as a *planetary nebula*. Later that year, Charles Messier observed this object and gave it number 57 in his catalog.

CYGNUS

High in the August sky is an easy constellation to recognize, called *Cygnus*, the Swan. The primary asterism of Cygnus looks very much like a cross. In fact, the constellation is sometimes referred to as the Northern Cross. The brightest star in Cygnus, *Deneb*, marks the eastern apex of the Summer Triangle.

Deneb

Deneb is a remarkable star. At magnitude 1.26, it looks like any of the other brighter stars, but of the 25 brightest stars, Deneb is the farthest from us. It is 1600 light-years away and if our sun was in Deneb's place,

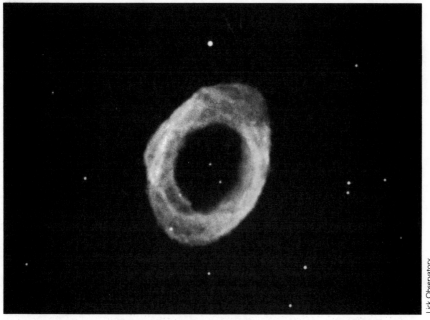

8-2 The Ring Nebula, M57, in Lyra.

the Sun would be a very faint thirteenth-magnitude star. Deneb is 60,000 times more luminous than the Sun. If it was located 32.5 light-years from Earth, it would shine at magnitude −7—15 times brighter than Venus and 100 times brighter than Sirius.

A familiar-looking nebula

If you can get away from the lights of the city, take a moment to look just east of Deneb. With the unaided eye, you might just be able to make out a bright patch of light. If you have a pair of binoculars handy, turn it on the patch and you will see a recognizable shape. It looks very much like an outline of North America, so it is called the *North American Nebula* (see FIG. 8-3).

The North American Nebula is an emission nebula. Like the gases in a neon sign, the nebula glows when the radiation from nearby stars "excites" it. The nebula is 1600 light-years away, about the same distance away as the luminous Deneb. Scientists think that Deneb is a prime source for the radiation needed to "turn on" the nebula.

VULPECULA

Tucked under the eastern wing of Cygnus is the small constellation of *Vulpecula*, the Fox. During the last week of September, this constellation is on the meridian at 9:00 P.M. (see FIG. 8-4).

8-3 The North American Nebula in Cygnus.

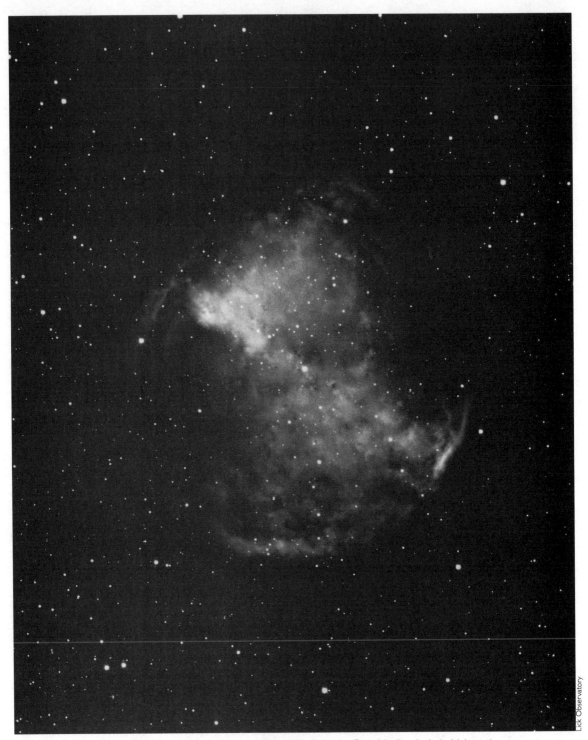

8-4 Another fine example of a planetary nebula is the Dumbbell nebula in Vulpecula.

AQUILA

South of Cygnus is the constellation of *Aquila*, the Eagle. Aquila is marked by the bright star, *Altair*, and its two nearby "attendants." Altair is the twelfth brightest star in the sky, and it shines at magnitude 0.7. It is about 16 light-years away, is 1.5 times the diameter of the Sun, and is 9 times more luminous than the Sun.

Aquila is a striking constellation because the Milky Way cuts through it prominently. On a dark night, away from the lights of the city, you can see the Milky Way mottled with dark "patches." These patches are called *dark nebulae* (see FIG. 8-5) and consist of dust that obscures whatever lies behind them.

During the early 1900s, an astronomer named E.E. Barnard made a study of these nebulae and cataloged over 300 of them. Like Messier's catalog, they all bear a letter designation (*B* for Barnard) and a number.

SCUTUM

Just south of Aquila is the small constellation of *Scutum*, the Shield. Scutum is a rather faint constellation, lost among the stars of the Milky Way. It is on the meridian during the beginning of September.

SAGITTA

Between Cygnus and Aquila is the small but distinct constellation of *Sagitta*. The constellation represents an arrow and it even looks like one! Sagitta is on the meridian during mid-September.

DELPHINUS

East of Sagitta and below Cygnus swims *Delphinus*, the Dolphin. With its diamond-shaped asterism, Delphinus is easy to pick out when it crosses the meridian during late September.

SAGITTARIUS

Skimming the southern horizon is another easily recognized constellation. *Sagittarius*, the Archer, could be called "the Teapot" because that is what its primary asterism looks like, complete with handle and spout! Sagittarius transits the meridian during late August and early September.

The Milky Way is quite dense in the area of Sagittarius. When we look in the direction of Sagittarius, we are looking toward the center of our own galaxy (see FIG. 8-6). It is rather difficult to see any real detail in this area because much of the galactic center is obscured by dust clouds. Looking toward the galactic center, we must peer through all the obscuring dust that forms our arm of the galaxy.

CAPRICORNUS

Located west of Sagittarius is the zodiacal constellation of *Capricornus*, the Sea Goat. This constellation looks very much like an arrowhead

8-5 Dark nebula can look plain or strikingly familiar: (A) B84,

(B) the Horsehead Nebula.

8-6 The Milky Way in Sagittarius near the Galactic Center.

pointed south. Capricornus is on the meridian at 9:00 P.M. during late September.

A PROJECT FOR THE YOUNG ASTRONOMER

The Milky Way is a magnificent sight as it stretches across the sky. Because our galaxy is so prominent in the late summer, an interesting project is to trace its pattern in the sky.

Detailed star charts show that the Milky Way extends into many constellations. After looking at several different star charts, you will notice that the boundaries of the Milky Way are never represented in quite the same way in any two charts. So, this project will test your ability to record the detail you see in the sky.

You must have dark skies for this project, so plan on doing it when you are away from the city lights. Next, take a trip to the library. Try to find a copy of *Norton's Star Atlas* or a copy of Wil Tirion's *Sky Atlas 2000.0.*

Begin by tracing the brighter stars and the Milky Way's borders. Use a regular dark pencil or felt-tip pen for the stars, but use a red pencil or red ink for the Milky-Way outline. While you are observing, these red lines will not show under the light from your red flashlight.

When you make your observations, use another color of pencil or marker to trace your own boundaries for the Milky Way. If you can't see your original tracing of the boundaries, it will not influence how you see the Milky Way on the night of your observation.

Begin your session by carefully recording the date, time, weather conditions, and anything else that you think will affect your observations. Next, carefully plot the outline of the Milky Way on your chart as you see it.

When you have completed your observation, and you are inside, compare the two. Which shows a greater extent of the Milky Way: the chart tracing or your outline? How much do they differ? What could be the cause of the difference? Enter all this information in your observation notebook.

It would be interesting to repeat this observation over a number of nights. Record your results each time and compare them. Can you offer an explanation as to why your outlines differ?

Chapter 9

Stars for an autumn evening

*A*s the year comes to an end, the sky has turned full circle. The stars that greeted us during January and February are beginning to rise earlier each month. This last group of stars, visible from October to December at 9:00 P.M., could be divided into three groups (see FIG. 9-1).

All of these constellations have something to do with water! First is the great "celestial sea," which runs along the southern horizon up to the equator. Aquarius is the Waterbearer, Pisces and Piscis Austrialis are fish, and Cetus is a sea monster.

The northern portion of the sky includes related constellations. Andromeda, Perseus, and the circumpolar constellations of Cassiopeia and Cepheus all played a role in the story of Andromeda and the Sea monster, Cetus. Some interpreters of the myth even include Pegasus in the story.

Finally, sprinkled among these star figures are small, but interesting constellations that are unrelated. Equuleus, and Lacerta are located along the western border of this section of sky. Aries, Triangulum, and Fornax are along the east, and Sculptor is along the southern horizon. The Milky Way runs along the northern tier of constellations stretching from east to west. It cuts through Lacerta, Cassiopeia, and Perseus.

AQUARIUS

Stretching below Pegasus is the zodiacal constellation of *Aquarius*, the Waterbearer. Aquarius is a large, but rather faint constellation. The primary asterism of Aquarius is called the *Water Jar* and is made up of three fourth-magnitude stars and a third-magnitude star (see FIG. 9-2). The fourth-magnitude stars form an equilateral triangle, and the third-magnitude star is in the center. The Water Jar transits the meridian at 9:00 P.M. during mid-October.

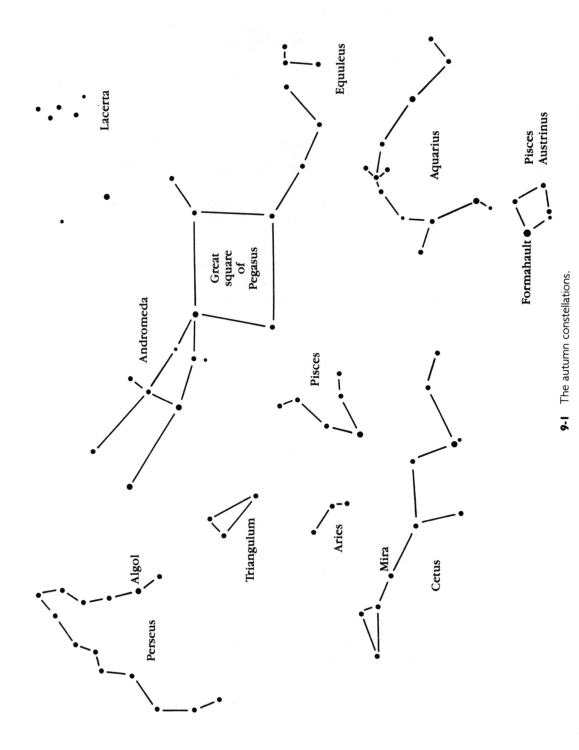

9-1 The autumn constellations.

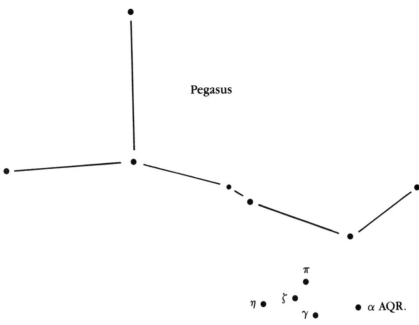

Pegasus

π

η • ζ •
γ •

• α AQR.

9-2 The asterism called the "Water Jar."

PISCES AUSTRINUS

South of Aquarius is the constellation of *Pisces Austrinus*, the Southern Fish. This star group contains mostly fourth-magnitude stars, except for Formalhaut, which shines at magnitude 1.19. Formalhaut is the southernmost bright star that can be seen from the midlatitudes of the United States. Formalhaut is on the meridian at October 20.

LACERTA

North of Pegasus and nestled under Cepheus is the small constellation of *Lacerta*, the Lizard. Made up of fourth-magnitude stars, Lacerta does have an asterism that is easy to identify, but the westward-pointing W might be hard to see under city skies. Lacerta is on the meridian at 9:00 P.M. during the beginning of October.

EQUULEUS

Just west of Pegasus is the small constellation of *Equuleus*, the Small Horse. Equuleus is easy to identify with its parallelogram-shaped asterism. Equuleus crosses the meridian at 9:00 P.M. during the beginning of October.

SCULPTOR

East of Piscis Austrinus is the constellation *Sculptor*, which represents a sculptor's tools. Sculptor does not have a prominent asterism, and it consists of faint stars. Sculptor transits the meridian during the first week of November.

ANDROMEDA

High in the sky at 9:00 P.M. during mid-November is *Andromeda*, the Chained Lady. This constellation is marked by a curving line of stars that begins at the northeast corner of neighboring Pegasus.

M31: as far as the unaided eye can see!

Andromeda contains many fascinating objects for the observer, but the most spectacular sight is the galaxy M31. Visible as a greenish glow, this object is about as far as you can see without some sort of optical aid! M31, also known as the Great Andromeda Galaxy, is 2.2 million light-years from us (see FIG. 9-3).

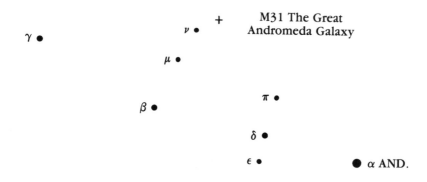

9-3 Location of M31, the Andromeda galaxy.

The Andromeda Galaxy was known to observers before the invention of the telescope. Persian astronomer Al Sufi described it as a "little cloud" in A.D. 986. Until early in the twentieth century, objects like the Andromeda Galaxy were thought to be part of our own Milky Way and were called *white nebulae*. It was not until 1924 that Edwin Hubble announced that Andromeda and the "little clouds" were distant collections of individual stars (see FIG. 9-4).

Like our Milky Way, M31 is a spiral galaxy. Recent measurements indicate that the Andromeda Galaxy is much larger than our Milky Way. Our galaxy is about 100,000 light-years across, while Andromeda is about 180,000 light-years across. Like our Galaxy, Andromeda has two companion galaxies, known as M32 and M110.

CETUS

From below Pisces on the west, to the area below Aries in the east, is the large constellation *Cetus*, the Sea Monster. The head of this sea creature, just below Aries, is marked by a circle of stars. Stretching west is a long, wandering line of stars that marks its body. Cetus is another large constellation. It crosses the meridian at 9:00 P.M. during mid-November (its "body") and early December (its "head").

Mira: the Wonderful star

Midway down the "neck" of Cetus is the star Omicron, known as *Mira* (see FIG. 9-5). In 1596, the Dutch astronomer David Fabricus observed

9-4 The Great Galaxy of Andromeda (M31).

91

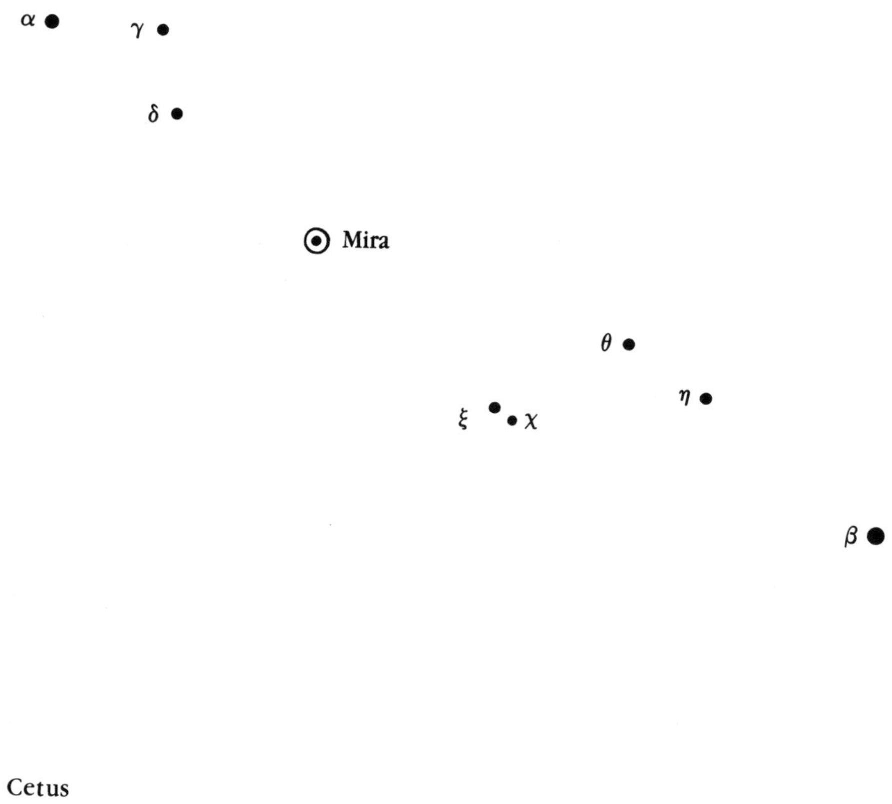

α •   γ •

δ •

◉ Mira

θ •

η •

ξ • •χ

β •

Cetus

9-5 Location of the Long-Period variable Mira Omicron Ceti.

what he thought was a nova at the location of Omicron. In 1603, the star-mapper Johann Bayer recorded Omicron as a fourth-magnitude star. Soon after his observation, Omicron mysteriously disappeared, only to reappear in about a year. As astronomers continued to observe Omicron, they noticed that the star was only visible a few weeks during the year. In the seventeenth century, there was no theory available to explain these variations and the star was labeled "Mira, the Wonderful."

Mira is what is called a *variable star*, a star that does not shine with a constant brightness, but varies over a given period of time. The brightest magnitude of the variable is called its *maxima*, and the faintest magnitude of the star is called its *minima*. The time it takes for the variable to go from one maxima to the next is called the star's *period*. Mira has a third-magnitude maxima and a tenth-magnitude minima. Its period is 331 days. The observed magnitudes of a variable are plotted on a chart known as a *light curve*.

Long-period variables

Mira has given its name to an entire class of variables. Mira-type variables are *long-period variables* (LPVs). Like the cepheids (see chapter 4), LPVs

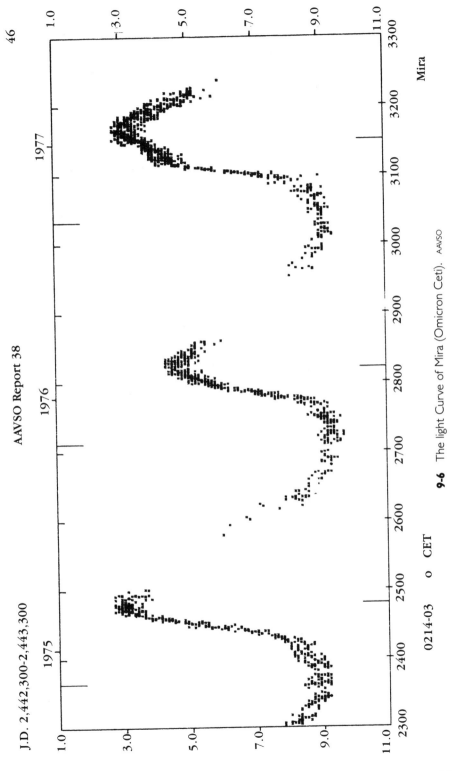

9-6 The light Curve of Mira (Omicron Ceti). AAVSO

expand and contract as they change in brightness. Unlike the Cepheids, however, they are not as precise in their fluctuations. Mira, for example, usually brightens to almost third-magnitude, but on a number of occasions, it has exceeded second-magnitude. In 1779, Mira almost reached first magnitude, becoming nearly as bright as Aldebaran in Taurus.

FORNAX

Near the southern horizon is the faint constellation of *Fornax*, the Furnace. There are no really bright stars in Fornax, and it transits the meridian at 9:00 P.M. in late December.

ARIES

South of Triangulum is the small but distinctive constellation of *Aries*, the Ram. Aries is marked by two relatively bright stars, Alpha and Beta, both about second magnitude. A third star, Gamma at fourth magnitude, forms a very sharp triangle with Alpha and Beta. Aries is on the meridian during the first week of December.

TRIANGULUM

South of Andromeda is *Triangulum*, the Triangle. Triangulum is another constellation that looks like its name. Alpha, Beta, and Gamma form the points of a dim, but recognizable, triangle. This constellation is on the meridian during early December.

Since Triangulum is a relatively faint constellation, try to observe it away from city lights. Under clear country skies, you might see a patchy glow of light, almost as big as the Full Moon, just north and west of Alpha. This is the spiral galaxy, *M33*. Slightly farther away than M31, M33 is about 2.4 million light-years away from us.

M33 is much more difficult to see than the Andromeda Galaxy. Although Andromeda presents itself to us at about a ''3/4'' profile, M33 is ''face on'' to us, looking like a celestial pinwheel (FIG. 9-7). M33 is invisible under city skies, even from a dark site. However, it hangs in the sky like a pale Moon when well away from light pollution.

PERSEUS

East of Andromeda is *Perseus*, the Hero. Perseus sits astride the Milky Way and is on the meridian at the end of December (see FIG. 9-8).

One of the most interesting stars in this constellation is *Algol*, Beta (β) Persei. Throughout history, Algol has been considered a ''bad-luck star.'' Observers in China, Greece, Rome, and Persia all noted that the star had a tendency to ''wink,'' and this was considered a sign of bad luck.

When you first observe Algol, it looks like any other second-magnitude star. However, if you watch over a period of 2.5 days, you will see it begin to dim, fading to magnitude 3.5 in 4 hours. It remains at magnitude 3.5 for 20 minutes before it returns to its former brightness of second-magnitude. The exact period of Algol to drop to its minimum

9-7 The spiral galaxy M33 in Triangulum.

9-8 The Double Cluster in Perseus is another fine example of open-star clusters.

Lick Observatory

brightness, return to second-magnitude, and then dim to its minimum again, is 2 days, 20 hours, 48 minutes, and 56 seconds.

Algol is a variable star. Astronomers in the eighteenth century were at a loss to explain Algol's behavior, until 1782. In that year, John Goodricke (1764-1786), born deaf and never able to speak, theorized that Algol was not a single star, but two. Today, we know that this is the reason behind Algol's "wink."

Algol is an example of an *eclipsing binary star*. The main component of the system, *Algol-A*, is a bright star, almost 100 times more luminous than the Sun. Around this star orbits another star, *Algol-B*, larger and "darker" than *A*. Every 2 days, 20 hours, 48 minutes, and 56 seconds, Algol-B passes between us and the primary, Algol-A. As *B* begins to pass in front of, or eclipse, *A*, the light from *A* begins to dim. Algol-B does not completely cover Algol-A; we see a partial eclipse. When Algol-B covers as much of Algol A as we can see, the star shines at magnitude 3.5. As it "slides" past Algol-A, uncovering the brighter star, we see it brighten back to second-magnitude (see FIG. 9-9).

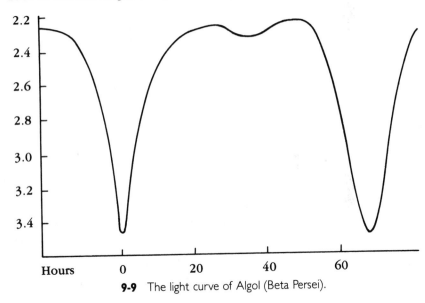

9-9 The light curve of Algol (Beta Persei).

PEGASUS

The most distinctive of the autumn constellations is *Pegasus*, the Flying Horse. Pegasus is marked by the large asterism called the *Great Square*. The western side of the Great Square is a pair of second-magnitude stars. The eastern edge of the asterism consists of a third-magnitude star and a star from Andromeda, second-magnitude Alpha.

Pegasus is a very large constellation. Its western section, representing the head of the flying horse, begins to transit the meridian during early October. The Great Square, which represents the body of the horse, reaches the meridian in early November.

PISCES

Wedged between Cetus to the south and Pegasus to the north is *Pisces*, the Fishes. Pisces is marked by a small asterism directly below the Great Square of Pegasus, called the Circlet. This constellation stretches east from the Circlet and takes the entire month of November to transit the meridian.

A PROJECT FOR THE YOUNG ASTRONOMER

You can do many projects that with nothing more than the unaided eye under the stars of autumn. Probably the most interesting project is to watch Algol change from minima to minima.

In order to undertake this project, all you will need is a spot to relax that will give you a clear view of Algol and its surrounding stars and a watch, pencil, and paper. You will also need to make a trip to your local library.

Most libraries subscribe to *Sky & Telescope* magazine. If yours does not, ask the librarian if he or she can add it to the library's list. Look up the feature section of the magazine, called the "Celestial Calendar." Once you find it, look for the smaller section labeled "Minima of Algol." Under this section will be a list of dates and times when Algol will be at minimum brightness.

The times listed in this section are for the *Universal Time* (UT) of the event. UT measures time on a 24-hour clock, beginning at midnight for the Greenwich Observatory in England. To convert these times to your local time, subtract 5 hours for Eastern Standard Time (EST), 6 hours for Central Standard Time (CST), 7 hours for Mountain Standard Time (MST), and 8 hours for Pacific Standard Time (PST). If you are presently under local daylight time, add an hour.

August 2, 1991, at 14 hours UT is equal to 8:00 A.M. EDT, 7:00 A.M. CDT, 6:00 A.M. MDT, and 5:00 A.M. PDT. If you do your subtraction and come up with a negative result, add 24 hours and subtract 1 day from the date of the event. For example, August 14, 1991, at 1 hour UT becomes 9:00 P.M. August *13* EDT.

Once you have one date for the minimum of Algol, you can begin your project. In order to find a rough idea of the next minimum, simply add 2.5 days to the figure you have. For example, on April 14, 1990, at 1:52 UT, Algol was at minimum light. This comes out to 7:52 CST for April 13. The next minimum should have taken place about 36 hours later (April 15 at about 7 A.M.). Determine if Perseus and Algol will be visible to you at this time. If they are, get your pencil, watch, and paper ready. If not, add another cycle and check again. Try to begin your observations while Algol is still at its maximum brightness.

When you have determined that Algol and the comparison stars (see FIG. 9-10) will be visible, the rest is easy. Record the time of your observation. Now notice which star is closest to Algol in brightness and record that magnitude. If you catch Algol dimming in magnitude, repeat these

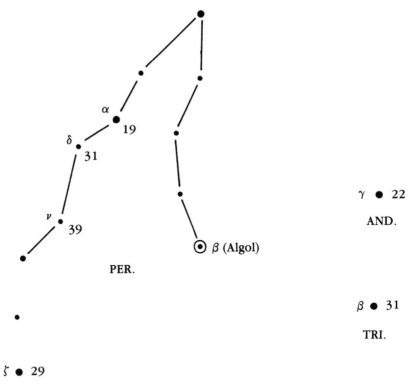

9-10 The comparison stars for Algol.

observations for a period of a few hours. After you are finished for the evening, go inside and plot your observations on a sheet of graph paper (see FIG. 9-11). You have created your own light curve for Algol. How closely does it compare to Fig. 9-7?

9-11 Create your own light curve for Algol. Plot the brightness along the vertical axis and the times along the horizontal axis.

Chapter 10

The southern stars

*T*here is another part of the sky that those of us living in the United States do not get to see. For us, the sky is defined by Polaris and its height above the northern horizon. For others, living in southern Texas, southern Florida, or Hawaii, just a glimpse of the beauty of the southern sky is visible (see FIG. 10-1).

Before the days when the great explorers sailed for the New World, the southern skies were a mystery. It is interesting that some of the constellations of the southern sky are not new at all. Some were known to astronomers because a portion peeked over the horizon. Also, the phenomenon of precession changes the location of the North Celestial Pole and the entire sky. Because of precession, many of the star figures now invisible to us once were prominent along the southern horizon.

In 1603, the German astronomer and starmapper Johann Bayer (1572-1625) created the first charts of the entire heavens. His work, called *Uranometria*, included, for the first time, constellations visible from both north and south of the equator. His work included the 48 constellations handed down from the Greek astronomers to which he added 12 new constellations in the Southern Hemisphere. In 1752, French astronomer Nicolas LaCaille (1713-1762) added another 14 constellations to the southern skies.

Our knowledge of the southern skies is rather limited because, until relatively recently, most of the world's major observatories were located in the Northern Hemisphere. It was not until the 1800s that astronomers started to erect telescopes in the Southern Hemisphere. Today, many countries are building observatories south of the equator, dedicated to studying the southern sky.

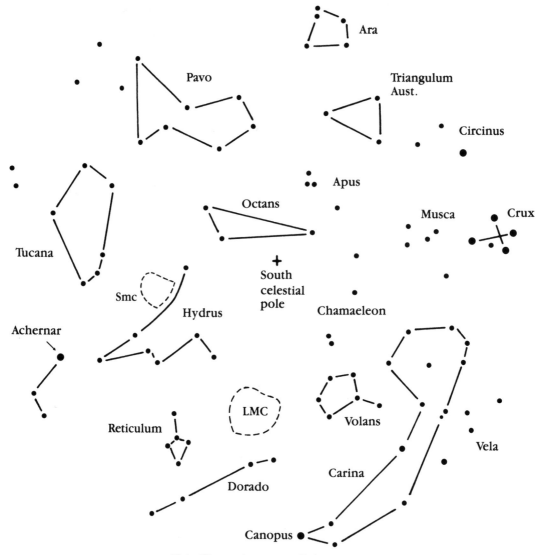

10-1 The southern constellations.

APUS

One of Bayer's 12 new constellations was *Apus*, the Bird of Paradise. Lying between Octans and Triangulum Australe, it does not contain any stars brighter than fourth-magnitude.

ARA

Another one of Bayer's constellations is *Ara*, the Altar. Directly below Scorpius, a small part of Ara can be seen low on the horizon from the mid-northern latitudes. Like many of the southern constellations, it does not contain any really bright stars; the brightest in this constellation is third-magnitude.

CARINA

Carina was once part of the great constellation *Argo Navis*. Argo represented the ship that Jason and the Argonauts sailed on in their quest for the Golden Fleece (which is represented by the constellation Aries). Argo was a huge constellation, and sections of it are still visible on the southern horizon. Carina, however, is the southernmost section of the "good ship" Argo. It can only be seen from very far south. Carina represents the keel of the ship.

Unlike many of the other southern constellations, Carina lies in an area of the sky rich in many types of objects. The Milky Way cuts through the northeast corner of the constellation, which is marked by a number of bright stars.

The brightest of the stars in Carina is *Canopus*. Canopus is the second brightest star in the heavens, shining at magnitude −0.7. Canopus is an F-type star. It is about 30 times the diameter of the Sun and some 1400 times more luminous than the Sun. Canopus is 74 light-years from the Sun.

CHAMAELEON

Bayer noted *Chamaeleon* on his map of 1603. The Chamaeleon is located between Carina and Octans. This constellation is made up of rather faint stars, the brightest of which is fourth-magnitude.

CIRCINUS

Located between Centaurus and Apus is *Circinus*, the Compasses. Added to the star charts by LaCaille, it represents the navigational compass. The brightest star in this small constellation is third-magnitude.

CRUX

Crux, the Southern Cross, is the smallest constellation in the skies. Once considered part of Centaurus, it was entered on Bayer's map of 1603 as a separate constellation.

Unlike many of the other southern constellations, Crux is a striking asterism. Its four bright stars do look like a cross, but to be honest, it looks more like a rhombus or lop-sided box. Its likeness can be found on the flags of many countries south of the equator.

The brightest star in the constellation is called *Acrux*. At magnitude 0.8, it marks the southern foot of the cross. The other three stars that make up the asterism are also bright. Beta, the eastern arm, is magnitude 1.2; Gamma, the top of the cross, is magnitude 1.6. The Milky Way runs through most of the constellation, making for spectacular viewing with both the unaided eye and binoculars. The combination of bright stars and the Milky Way makes Crux one of the most striking sights in the sky.

DORADO

Dorado, the Swordfish, was first drawn by Bayer in his *Uranometria*. It would be a rather insignificant constellation, except for a starry cloud on its southern border. This starry cloud was first observed by Portuguese sailors during the fifteenth century. Later, it was named for the explorer Ferdinand Magellan and called the *Large Magellanic Cloud* (LMC). The LMC is more than a starry cloud; it is a nearby galaxy and a "companion" to our Milky Way. The LMC is about 190,000 light-years away and 50,000 light-years across.

Early in 1987, a supernova flared in the LMC. Called *1987A*, the light we saw was caused by an explosion that took place over 180,000 years ago. It was the first bright supernova seen in a nearby galaxy in almost 100 years.

Supernovae come in two types. *Type II* supernovae, like Tycho's Star, are caused when a massive star develops an "onion skin" of layers of material that eventually collapse in a massive explosion.

Type I supernovae, like 1987A, occur when material is exchanged between the two components of a double star. The smaller, more massive component draws material from the larger component. As the material builds up on the smaller star, usually a white dwarf, it reaches a point when the extra material on the star causes unbelievable crushing pressures. The white dwarf then heats up dramatically and explodes.

GRUS

Many of the southern constellations noted on star charts by Bayer took the form of birds. *Grus*, another of his additions, represents a crane. Grus lies north of Tucana and south of Pisis Austrinus.

HOROLOGIUM

LaCaille added Horologium to represent a clock in 1752. It is located between Eridanus and Hydrus, but it contains no prominent asterism or bright star.

HYDRUS

Noted by Bayer on his 1603 map, Hydrus lies between Eridanus and Octans. It represents another sea monster, like Hydra and Ceteus in the northern skies.

INDUS

Indus is another of the constellations added by Bayer to the uncharted southern skies. Indus represents the inhabitants of the New World.

MENSA

LaCaille added this constellation to the star charts in 1752. Mensa represents Table Mountain outside Cape Town, South Africa, where much of the early research of the southern skies was done during the eighteenth century. Mensa lies between Octans and Dorado, and contains a portion of the Large Magellanic Cloud.

MICROSCOPIUM

Located just south of Capricornus is Microscopium, which LaCaille drew to represent a microscope.

MUSCA

This constellation was first listed in 1603 on Bayer's *Uranometria* under a different name. Bayer called it *Apis*, the Bee, and it was known by that name until 1752. That year LaCaille changed the name of the constellation to *Musca*, the Fly. This constellation lies between Crux and Chamaeleon. The Milky Way runs through the portion of the constellation that is adjacent to Crux.

NORMA

Norma is a small constellation of faint stars immersed in the Milky Way. It was drawn by LaCaille in 1752 to represent a carpenter's level.

OCTANS

Added to the charts by LaCaille in 1752, *Octans* is the location of the South Celestial Pole (SCP). Unlike the NCP, there is no bright star near the SCP to help you find it. The star nearest to the SCP, Sigma Octantis, is only 1 degree away, but it is only fifth-magnitude. Also, there is no real asterism, like the Big Dipper, to point the way to the SCP.

PAVO

Pavo, the Peacock, was created by Bayer in 1603. It lies between Telescopium and Octans. Unfortunately, it contains only one bright star, the second-magnitude Alpha.

PHOENIX

Another of the bird constellations of the southern sky is *Phoenix*, the fabled bird that would rise from its own ashes. Bayer found this constellation in an area of the southern sky that is bordered on the south by Tucana, the west by Grus, the east by Eridanus, and the north by Sculptor.

PICTOR

Pictor, the Painter's Easel, was first drawn by LaCaille in 1752. Located south of Columba, Pictor contains few stars and is difficult to recognize.

RETICULUM

LaCaille created *Reticulum* to honor another of the inventions of the scientific world, the reticle. It lies between Dorado and Horolgium. Its brightest star is third-magnitude Alpha.

TELESCOPIUM

LaCaille wanted to commemorate many of the scientific instruments of his day with constellations in the sky, particularly in the southern sky. This constellation is a salute to the instrument most used by astronomers, both amateur and professional. *Telescopium*, unfortunately, is a rather barren-looking constellation. Most of the stars found within its borders are faint—fifth-magnitude and fainter. An asterism containing three fourth-magnitude stars is in the northwest corner of the constellation. Telescopium is located just south of Corona Australis and Sagittarius.

TRIANGULUM AUSTRALE

Triangulum Australe, the Southern Triangle, is marked by a triangle of second- and third-magnitude stars. Located between Apus to the south and Norma to the north, Triangulum Australe is an easy southern constellation to find.

TUCANA

Another of Bayer's constellations is *Tucana*, the Toucan. This constellation rests between Phoenix and Octans. Within the constellation's boundaries lies the other companion galaxy to our Milky Way, the *Small Magellanic Cloud* (SMC), an irregularly shaped galaxy about 190,000 light-years from us.

VELA

Vela was once part of the giant *Argo Navis*. This constellation represents the sails of Jason's ship and sits north of Carina. Portions of Vela are visible from the Northern Hemisphere, but these sections are very low on the southern horizon.

VOLANS

Created by Bayer, *Volans*, the Flying Fish, is not a very prominent constellation. The brightest stars in Volans are only fourth-magnitude. It is located between Carina and Mensa.

Chapter **11**

The beacon
of the night

*T*he brightest and easiest to find nighttime object is the Moon. It was probably the first object Galileo turned his telescope toward. The drawings of his observations, recorded in his book *Sidereus Nuncius* (The Starry Messenger), show a strange world. It looks barren, rocky, and pitted with craters.

PHASES

The first thing you notice about the Moon is its phases (see FIG. 11-1). The Moon takes a little over 27 days to complete one orbit of the Earth, with respect to the background stars. This is called the Moon's *sidereal period*. The time it takes for lunar phases to repeat, first quarter to first quarter, is called the Moon's *synodic period*, and it runs about 29.5 days. Why this difference? As the Moon orbits the Earth, the Earth orbits the Sun. Because of this combination of motion, it takes additional time for the Earth-Moon-Sun trio to form the same geometry to repeat a particular phase. Because of this orbital geometry, the Moon rises about 45 minutes later each night.

In addition to revolving around the Earth, the Moon rotates on its axis. The Moon has what is called a *captured rotation*. It completes one rotation of its axis in the time that it takes to make one revolution of the Earth. As a result, we would expect to be able to see only 50 percent of the lunar surface, but like many other things in the night sky, the Moon has a few surprises in store for us. As it moves around the Earth in its orbit, the Moon wobbles. This wobble, called *libration*, turns the Moon ever so slightly, so we can look around its edge (see FIG. 11-2). So instead of being able to see 50 percent of the surface, we can see a bit more—59 percent to be exact.

The phases we see from Earth are the result of the changing relationship between the Sun and Moon caused by the Sun's illumination of the

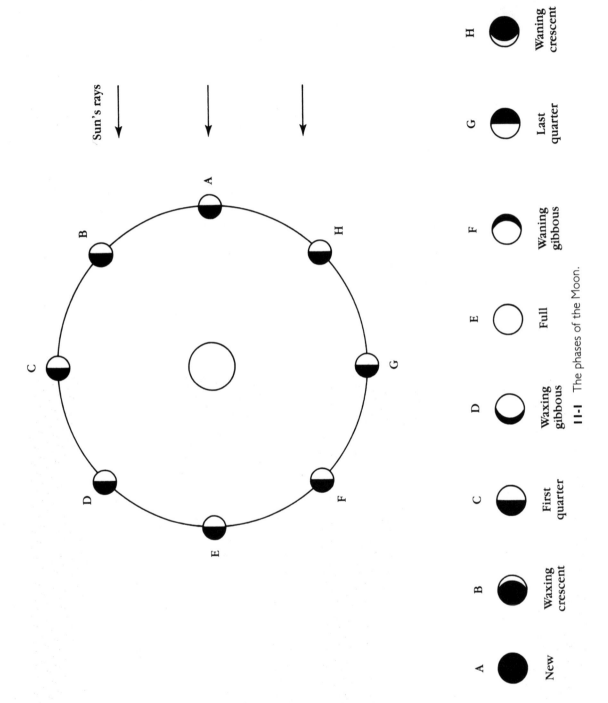

11-1 The phases of the Moon.

11-2 Libration of the Moon.

Moon, and not its lunar rotation. When the Moon is new, the Sun is beginning to climb into the lunar sky. The line that separates the dark from the light portion of the Moon is called the *terminator*, and it marks the sunrise line. As the lunar day progresses, the Sun rises higher in the lunar sky until it is directly overhead (noon) of the lunar surface. This is Full Moon. As the Sun sinks toward the lunar horizon, the terminator becomes the sunset line. Features near the terminator are illuminated by the low Sun, throwing long, dark shadows across the lunar surface.

The best time to observe any feature on the Moon, with a few exceptions, is when the terminator is nearby. When the Moon is full, the Sun is overhead and throwing no shadows, making it difficult to see any surface detail.

Just after New Moon, an interesting phenomenon occurs. You can see the thin crescent Moon hanging low in the sky. Notice that the section of the Moon that is "dark" is not completely invisible; it looks as if it is glowing. This phenomenon is often called "the New Moon in the Old Moon's arms," or *earthshine*. The reflection of light from the Earth illuminates the darkened section of the Moon. If you look at the Moon with a pair of binoculars or a small telescope, you can see some features that will not be visible for some weeks to come.

CRATERS AND SEAS

When you look at the Moon, you will notice that it has two types of terrain. The darker areas are called *maria*, or "seas" (see FIG. 11-3). They are not really seas, but rather flat, dark plains of lava. The theory that the mare (plural for maria) contain water dates back to very early times. Early astronomers looked at the Moon and thought they were seeing a reflection of the Earth's surface. The dark areas, they reasoned, were the images of the seas. Mare are found primarily on the northern hemisphere of the Moon.

11-3 Mare Serenitatis.

The other type of terrain found on the Moon is called *highland*. These are the bright areas and contain a variety of craters, mountains, ridges, and cracks (see FIG. 11-4).

The dominant features on the Moon are the craters. Found all over the lunar surface, craters are the result of volcanic action or impacts by chunks of rock. Craters range in size from *Bailly*, measuring 183 miles, down to microscopic dimples in the lunar surface.

Lick Observatory

11-4 A section of the southern highlands.

A PROJECT FOR THE YOUNG ASTRONOMER:
What can you see?

Because the Moon is so close to Earth, a mere 0.25 million miles away, you can see more detail on its surface than most telescopes show of other planets. All of the mare and many of the larger craters are easily visible to the unaided eye or with a good pair of binoculars.

A good time to begin your observation of the Moon is a few days after New Moon. Features will become visible as they near the terminator. Using your unaided eye or a small pair of binoculars, try to locate each of the features mentioned in this section.

Visible just after sunset is the crescent of the four-day-old Moon (see FIG. 11-5). Easily visible are two of the lunar mare. *Mare Crisium*, the Sea of Crises, is an elliptically shaped lava plain 270 by 350 miles. Inside its borders is a small crater in the southwest corner, called *Picard*. Picard is 16 miles across the 7600 feet deep. Directly south of Mare Crisium is *Mare Fecunditatis*, the Sea of Fertility. This mare covers about 150,000 square miles of lunar surface and looks rather boxlike.

When the Moon is seven days old, it is at *first quarter* (see FIG. 11-6). A wealth of detail is now visible along the terminator. Three more mare are prominently visible. The first is found in the center of the quarter Moon. *Mare Tranquillitatis*, the Sea of Tranquillity, is 400 by 550 miles.

Located to the northwest of Mare Tranquillitatis is *Mare Serenitatis*, the Sea of Serenity, measuring 360 by 420 miles. Inside Mare Serenitatis are two small craters. Measuring 10 miles across, *Bessel* is set out by a white streak that is very apparent to the unaided eye. Another small crater in this mare is *Linne*. It lies on a white spot 7 miles across. The contrast of the white on the dark floor of the mare should make this feature easily visible. Can you see Linne with your unaided eyes or do you need a pair of binoculars?

Just south of Mare Tranquillitatis is *Mare Nectaris*, the Sea of Nectar, which is 220 by 260 miles. Located on the western "shore" of Mare Nectaris is the crater *Theophilus*, which is 65 miles across and 22,000 feet deep.

Along the terminator of the seven-day Moon are a number of distinct craters. How many of them can you see without optical aid? To the north and slightly east of the terminator is *Aristotle*, a crater 55 miles across. Just south of this crater is *Eudoxus*, roughly 40 miles across. South of these craters, almost at the center of the terminator, is the crater *Manilius*. This crater is 25 miles across. The crater sits on the floor of *Mare Vaporum*, the Sea of Vapors, and should stand out quite well. These craters run in size from 55 miles across down to 1 mile across. They should be a good test of your visual ability.

When the Moon is ten days old, more of it becomes visible (see FIG. 11-7). *Mare Imbrium*, the Sea of Rains, is visible in the north. An oval-shaped plain, 670 by 750 miles, Mare Imbrium is home to some of the most striking features on the Moon. Along the northern border of the Mare is the crater *Plato*, which is 64 by 67 miles. Plato is easily seen throughout the lunar "day." Its dark floor contrasts with the bright background found at Full Moon. Visible against the dark floor of the mare should be the crater *Archimedes*, which is 51 miles across.

Coming into view is the largest of the lunar plains. *Oceanus Procellarum*, the Ocean of Storms, is 1200 miles across. Found on this vast plain

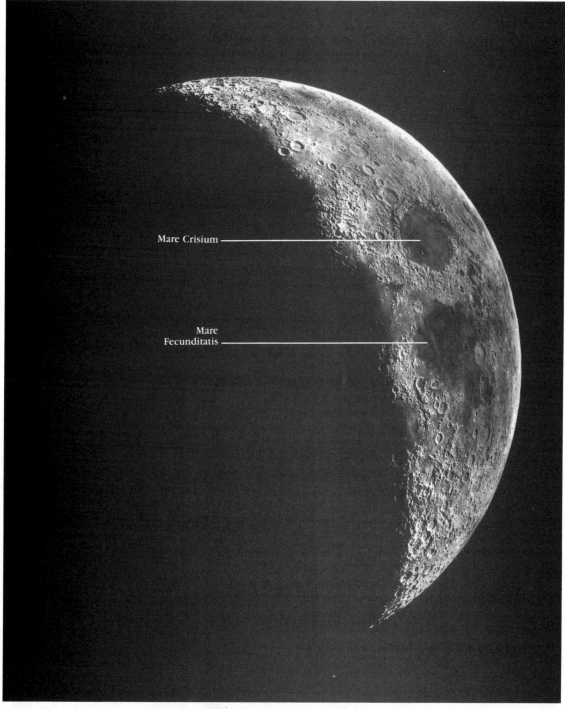

Mare Crisium ———————————

Mare
Fecunditatis ———————————

11-5 The four-day-old Moon.

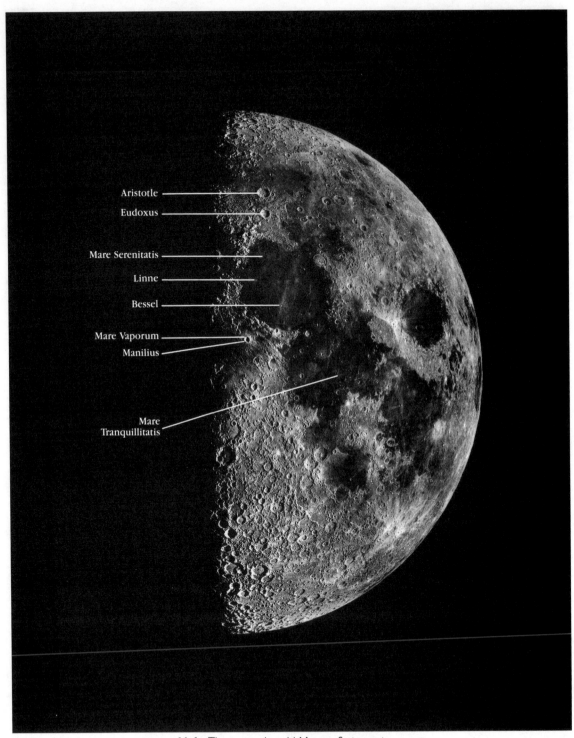

Aristotle

Eudoxus

Mare Serenitatis

Linne

Bessel

Mare Vaporum

Manilius

Mare
Tranquillitatis

11-6 The seven-day-old Moon—first quarter.

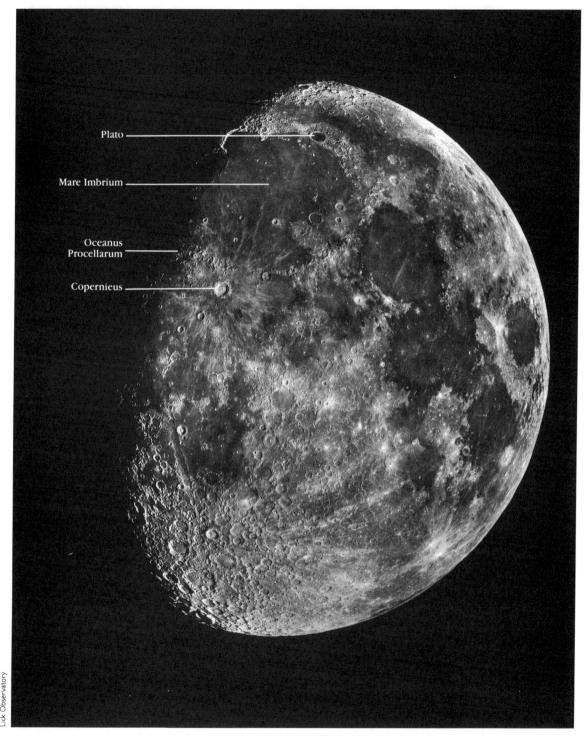

Plato

Mare Imbrium

Oceanus
Procellarum

Copernieus

11-7 The ten-day-old Moon.

Aristoarchus

Kepler

Copernicus

Tycho

11-8 Full Moon.

is the interesting crater *Copernicus*. As the Sun rises over the 60-mile crater, you can see it quite plainly on the lunar surface. During the period when the crater is under high illumination, however, its shape is lost and it appears as a bright patch.

The Full Moon (FIG. 11-8) is a bit disappointing to look at. Many people think that the Full Moon would be the best time to observe our satellite, but this is not true. Because the Sun is overhead, as seen from the Moon, there are no shadows and most of the surface features appear washed out.

Full Moon is the best time to observe the mysterious *ray systems* that criss-cross the Moon, however. These features are strikingly apparent when the Moon is full. They appear as bright streaks that seem to originate from specific craters, like spokes on a wheel.

The most prominent ray system is centered around the crater *Tycho* (FIG. 11-9) in the southern highlands; it extends across the entire face of the Moon. Try to trace the complete Tycho ray system across the Moon.

11-9 A closeup of Tycho.

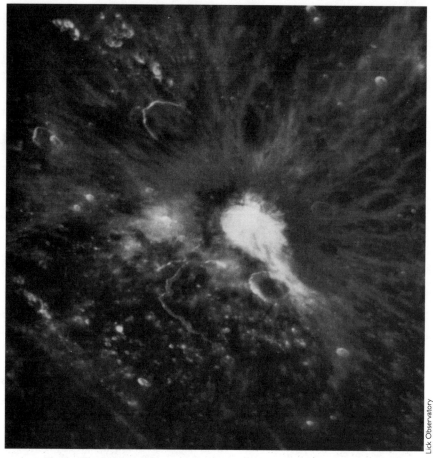

Lick Observatory

11-10 The brightest spot on the lunar surface, the crater Aristarchus.

Other prominent ray systems originate around the craters Copernicus and Kepler. Can you trace their trails?

Finally, the Full Moon offers us a chance to see the brightest spots on the Moon. West of Copernicus is the crater *Kepler*. This is a very bright object on the Moon, even though it is only 20 miles in diameter. North and west of Kepler is the brightest spot on the Moon, the crater *Aristarchus* (see FIG. 11-10). It is estimated that this 25-mile crater is one of the youngest on the Moon, only 50 million years old. Scientists think the crater is so bright because the impacting body that created it broke through a crust billions of years old. This crust has been darkened by exposure to solar radiation. Just below this crust was lighter-colored material, which was exposed from the impact.

Compare Copernicus, Kepler, and Aristarchus. Which spot appears brighter to you?

Chapter **12**

The family
of the sun

*T*he ancient astronomers called them *wanderers* because, unlike the "fixed" stars, they changed their position from night to night. We call them *planets* and they are the "children" of the Sun.

The planets follow the Sun through the sky. The path of the Sun, called the *ecliptic*, is also the path of the planets through the night sky. Although the ecliptic traces the exact path of the Sun through the sky, the planets wander north or south of the ecliptic, appearing to dance around the Sun.

As the planets orbit the Sun, their position with respect to the Earth changes. Planets with orbits inside the orbit of Earth (Mercury and Venus) are called *inferior planets* (see FIG. 12-1). Planets with orbits outside the orbit of the Earth (Mars to Pluto) are called *superior planets* (see FIG. 12-2). The period of time when a planet is visible in the sky is called an *apparition*.

MERCURY

The planet closest to the Sun is *Mercury*. It is a small planet, slightly larger than 3000 miles in diameter. Mercury is 36 million miles from the Sun, and it takes 88 days to complete one orbit.

Even though Mercury reaches magnitude −1.9 at its brightest, it is a very elusive object for the skywatcher to locate. Because it is so close to the Sun, it never really escapes from the Sun's glare. Shifting from the morning to evening sky, Mercury is almost always low on the horizon.

The best chance to see Mercury is when it is farthest from the Sun, as seen from Earth. This takes place when the planet reaches either its western or eastern elongation. *Western elongations* appear in the morning before sunrise, and *eastern elongations* appear in the evening after sunset. Apparitions are recorded for Mercury and Venus as being a morning

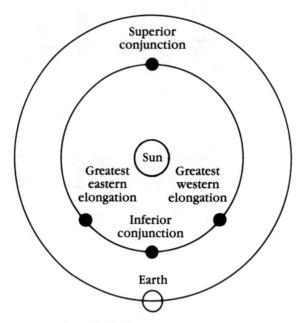

12-1 The orbit of an inferior planet.

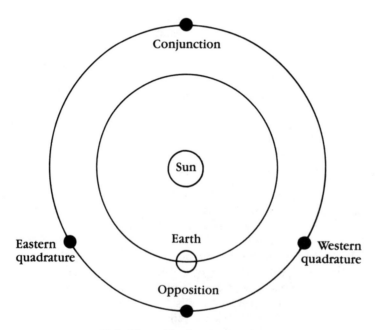

12-2 The orbit of a superior planet.

apparition (western elongation) or an evening apparition (eastern elongation). Eastern elongations are best observed when they occur during the spring; western elongations are best observed in the autumn.

Mercury has a very odd-looking orbit, and it is farthest, Mercury is only 28 degrees from the Sun. Because of this orbit, we are only able to see the planet two hours before sunrise or two hours after sunset. As the Sun moves toward the horizon, it will be very bright in the area where the Sun has set or will rise. This area is where you will have to look for Mercury.

As an inferior planet, Mercury shows phases like the Moon. When it is farthest from the Earth at superior conjunction, it appears as a small "full Mercury." At each of the elongations, it appears as a "quarter Mercury." At inferior conjunction, when it is closest to Earth, it appears as a thin crescent (see FIG. 12-3).

A project for the young astronomer

Mercury is a challenge to locate in the twilight sky. This project involves finding Mercury and plotting its position in the sky over the course of an apparition.

Simply locating Mercury in the morning or evening sky is a challenge in itself. Once you have found it, for how many days can you keep the planet under observation? Make a rough sketch of your eastern (or western) horizon and plot the location of the planet in relation to objects on the horizon. Use objects like trees, houses, or telephone poles as reference points. If you have access to a pair of binoculars, observe the planet. Can you detect any indication of the phases of Mercury?

VENUS

Second out from the Sun is Venus. The orbit of Venus averages about 68 million miles from the Sun, and it takes Venus about 225 days to complete one orbit. Venus is the Earth's nearest planetary neighbor. When the two are closest, only 26 million miles separate them. Like Mercury, Venus shows distinct phases.

For many years, scientists thought that Venus was a "twin" to the Earth. It has a diameter of 7600 miles, very close in size to the Earth's. The space-age soon showed those thoughts to be far from reality. Venus is a hothouse world. Surrounded by thick clouds, the surface temperature of Venus hovers around a "balmy" 800°F.

A project for the young astronomer

Venus is the brightest object in the sky outside of the Sun and Moon. Shining at magnitude − 4.5, at its brightest, Venus is visible during the day. Can you find the planet during the day?

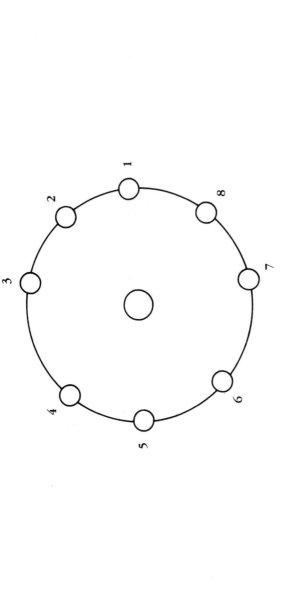

Phases + Relative Apparent Size of Inferior Planet

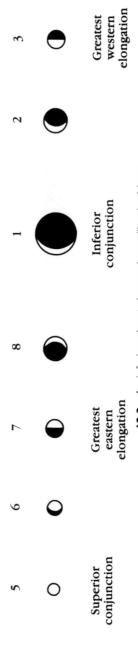

12-3 An inferior planet shows phases like the Moon.

Begin by observing the planet during the morning (or evening). Note where the planet is in relation to the Sun. Is it above or below the Sun and the imaginary line that runs through the Sun's center? During a morning (western) apparition, Venus will be "leading" the Sun across the sky. However, in the evening (eastern) apparitions, the planet "follows" the Sun.

Once you have an idea of where Venus is located in relation to the Sun, estimate when it will be highest in the sky near the meridian. Then carefully search the area of the sky where Venus should be.

MARS

The first planet outside the orbit of the Earth is Mars. Mars takes about 690 days to complete a single eccentric orbit around the Sun. Although the planet is an average distance of 141 million miles from the Sun, it comes as close as 129 million miles (its perihelion) and as far as 154 million miles (its aphelion).

Every two years or so, Mars makes a close approach to the Earth (see FIG. 12-4). Depending on where the Earth catches up with Mars, the Red Planet can come within 35 and 60 million miles of us.

The brightness of Mars varies tremendously over the course of an apparition. At its dimmest, Mars can have a magnitude of only 1.5. But as Mars closes the distance with Earth, Mars can grow in brightness to magnitude −2.6. The Red Planet will look like a red star, outshining everything in the sky, except Jupiter, Venus, the Moon, and the Sun. During very favorable apparitions, it will even become brighter than Jupiter.

Even though it is a small planet—only 4200 miles in diameter—Mars has been the subject of more interest than any other planet in the Solar System. In the 1870s, a debate began about the existence of intelligent life on the planet. Italian astronomer Giovanni Schiaparelli noticed what appeared to be straight lines on the planet. He called these lines *canali*, and the press and public immediately changed this to *canals*.

For the next few decades, the debate raged. In the 1890s, Percival Lowell established Lowell Observatory to study Mars and published many books on the "race of beings" who built the "canals" to save the water-poor Red Planet. It was not until the Mariner 4 mission of 1964 that the controversy was settled. The spacecraft returned with 22 photos of the planet that showed a crater-scarred surface but no canals (see FIG. 12-5).

As the first superior planet, Mars presents us with an opportunity to view the *retrograde motion* of a planet in its orbit. As the Earth moves in its orbit, it passes and is passed by the other planets of the Solar System. When seen from Earth, the planets that we are passing make little "loops" against the background stars as we pass them in our orbit. It looks as if the planet we are passing stops and moves backward along its orbit for a brief period of time (see FIG. 12-6). All the planets show a retrograde motion, but Mercury and Venus have their motion hidden because they are visible during twilight when the background stars are washed out by the Sun's glare. Mars, Jupiter, and Pluto show obvious loops. Saturn,

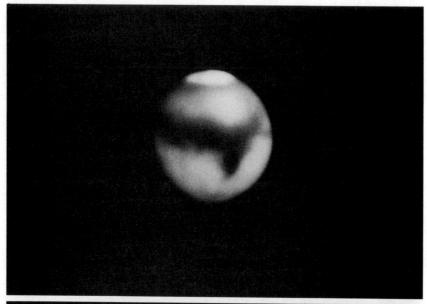

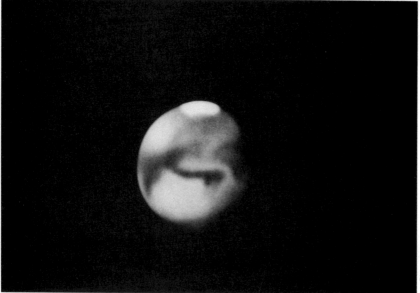

Lick Observatory

12-4 Mars during its 1971 apparition.

Uranus, and Neptune seem to back up along their own paths with little or no looping.

A project for the young astronomer

This project will take a bit of time to complete. First, a trip to the library is in order. Check a copy of *Astronomy* or *Sky & Telescope* magazine for the positions of Mars during the apparition you will be recording. Then get a

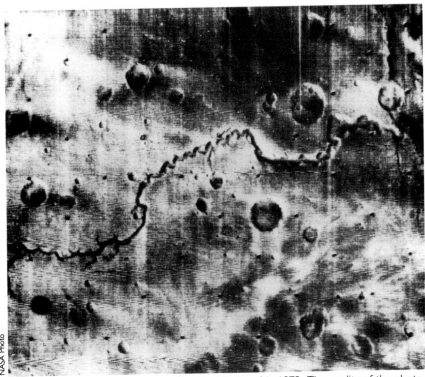

12-5 Surface of Mars as photographed by *Mariner 9* in 1972. The quality of the photographic images increased significantly over the first *Mariner 4* photos from 1964.

copy of *Norton's* or *SkyAtlas* and make an overlay of the area of the sky in which Mars will be located. Each night, you should record the position of Mars against the background stars. Over the course of the apparition, you will have a chart showing Mars and its retrograde loop.

JUPITER

Fifth from the Sun is Jupiter. With a diameter of 88,000 miles, Jupiter is the largest planet in the Solar System. Jupiter orbits the Sun at an average distance of 480 million miles and takes almost 12 Earth years for it to complete one orbit.

Jupiter is easy to spot in the night sky. Shining at magnitude −2.0 or brighter, Jupiter is usually the brightest "star" in the sky.

Galileo discovered a small "solar system" when he observed Jupiter in 1610 (FIG. 12-7). The four Galilean satellites would be visible to the unaided eye if it were not for Jupiter's glare. If you look for it, you can see the outermost of the Galileans, Callisto, with the unaided eye.

A project for the young astronomer

When Jupiter is high in the sky, look for Callisto. Carefully look for a faint "star" next to the planet. You might have to block out the glare of the

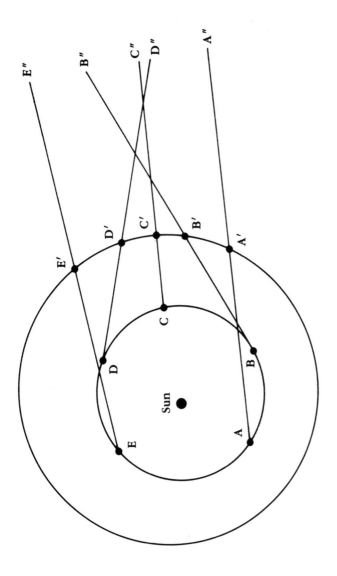

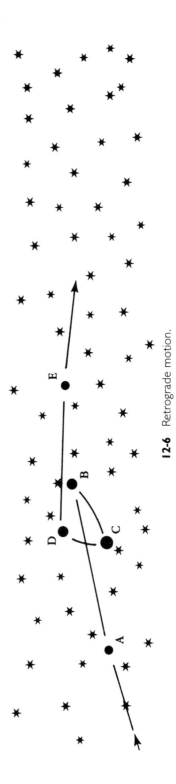

12-6 Retrograde motion.

12-7 Jupiter and its four bright Galilean satellites.

I — Io
II — Europa
III — Ganymede
IV — Callisto

planet with a pencil held at arm's length. Record the position of the star, if you see it, in your notebook. Later, check in a current copy of *Astronomy* or *Sky & Telescope* to see if the satellite is in that area.

Another project you can do requires a good pair of binoculars or a small telescope. With even the smallest of instruments, all four of the satellites should be visible. Observe the planet throughout a month or so and record the positions of each of the satellites.

SATURN

The last planet known to the ancients was *Saturn* (see FIG. 12-8). The Sixth Planet, orbiting some 886 million miles from the Sun, Saturn is the "showpiece" of the Solar System. Saturn appears as a yellow "star" in the night sky. Saturn will grow in brightness through its apparition from magnitude 1.5 to magnitude 0.

The fact that Saturn is the second-largest planet in the Solar System is overshadowed by the magnificent rings surrounding the planet. Composed of particles of rocks and ice, the rings of Saturn are a popular target for small telescopes. When Galileo first observed Saturn, he was puzzled by what he saw. His telescope, although "state of the art" for his time, was not able to show the rings clearly. He described it as a "three-lobed planet," and not until Christian Huygens observed the planet some 50 years later was the true beauty of the planet revealed.

A project for the young astronomer

This project requires the use of binoculars. Simply observe the planet with your binoculars and see if you can distinguish the rings of Saturn. If you have access to various sizes of binoculars, begin with the smallest pair and check the planet until you can see the rings.

URANUS

Until 1781, Saturn was marked as the end of the Solar System. In that year, William Herschel, an amateur astronomer in Bath, England, turned his homemade telescope on a star field in Gemini and became the first person to discover a planet.

The discovery of Uranus effectively "doubled" the size of the known Solar System. Orbiting at a distance of 1.8 billion miles, Uranus needs 84 Earth years to complete one revolution of the Sun.

12-8 Saturn and its rings.

A project for the young astronomer

Uranus, shining at magnitude 5.7, is at the border of visibility with the unaided eye. Check a recent copy of *Astronomy* or *Sky & Telescope* magazine for the current location of the planet. Using a copy of one of the star atlases mentioned earlier, record the stars in the area of the sky where the planet is. Observe the area and check each star you see against the plot you made from the atlas. If you come across a "star" that is not listed, that could be Uranus. The only way to tell for sure is to reexamine the area a few nights later. If the "star" has moved, you can record that you observed Uranus with the unaided eye.

NEPTUNE

Eighth from the Sun is Neptune. Neptune has the distinction of being the first planet to be discovered with a piece of paper. After the discovery of Uranus, astronomers tried to calculate its orbit. They worked diligently to predict just where Uranus would appear on a given night—but something was wrong. Uranus was never exactly where they predicted it would be. Something was out there, a "phantom" planet, they reasoned, that changed the orbit of Uranus slightly.

In 1845 and 1846, astronomers in different parts of the world came up with the possible location in the night sky of this "phantom" planet. The English mathematician John C. Adams and the French astronomer Urbain Le Verrier both predicted where the planet could be found. The German astronomer J.G. Galle pointed the telescope of the Berlin Observatory at the spot in space predicted by the two mathematicians and, sure enough, there was Neptune!

Neptune orbits the Sun at a distance of 2.8 billion miles, 30 times the distance between the Earth and the Sun. At that distance, it takes the planet 165 Earth years to complete one orbit! Neptune is beyond the unaided eye—shining at magnitude 7.7.

A project for the young astronomer

Neptune lies just beyond the reach of the unaided eye and needs some kind of optical aid to be found. What is the smallest instrument you need to find Neptune?

This project combines what you practiced when finding Saturn's rings and Uranus. Check for the position of the planet and prepare a set of charts. Use various sizes of binoculars, if they are available, to scan for Neptune. As with your unaided-eye search for Uranus, record any "suspect" star on your charts and check back a few nights later.

PLUTO

Last from the Sun is the strange, cold world of Pluto (see FIG. 12-9). Discovered in 1930, Pluto is the smallest of the planets. With a diameter of a mere 1200 miles, Pluto is smaller than the Earth's moon. At magnitude 13 or fainter, a telescope of at least 10 inches in aperture is necessary in order to see it.

COMETS AND METEORS

The planets are not the only members of the Sun's family. Smaller bodies also orbit in this gravity. Comets, composed of rock and ice, occasionally sweep in from the fringes of the Solar System (see FIG. 12-10). Comets are notoriously fickle. Comet Kohoutek (1973) and Comet Austin (1990) were both predicted to be extremely bright, spectacular objects. Both fizzled. Bright naked-eye comets are rare, but they do occur in our skies. Most comets attain a brightness that makes them suitable only for observing with a pair of binoculars or a small telescope.

Floating through the Solar System are particles of rock and dust that occasionally collide with Earth's atmosphere. In space, these are called *meteoroids*. When they hit the Earth's atmosphere, they become *meteors*, and we see them as streaks of light in the night sky. If they are large enough to survive the blazing trip through the atmosphere and land on Earth, they are called *meteorites*.

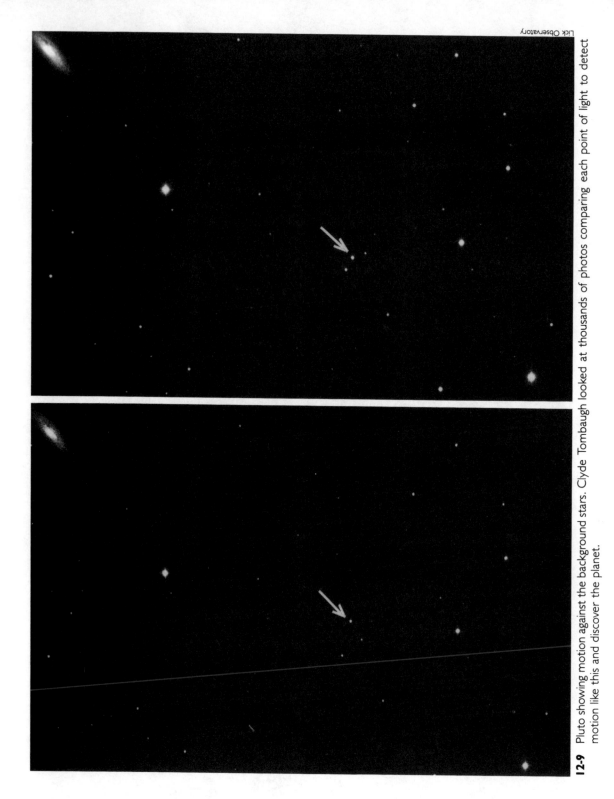

12-9 Pluto showing motion against the background stars. Clyde Tombaugh looked at thousands of photos comparing each point of light to detect motion like this and discover the planet.

12-10 The Comet Bradfield.

Meteors can be seen on any night of the year. On an average night, an observer will see about five meteors per hour. These are called *sporadic meteors*. Sporadic meteors are the result of random collisions of these interplanetary dust particles with the Earth. As the Earth revolves around the Sun, it sweeps up dust and debris that become meteors.

Meteors also can be associated with *meteor showers*. Meteor showers occur when the Earth encounters large "clouds" of dust and debris. Many of the "clouds" are associated with comets—they are either the remnants of a comet or a cloud traveling with the comet. As the Earth sweeps through this cloud of dust, the hourly rate of visible meteors can increase from five per hour to hundreds per hour.

Meteor showers seem to originate from specific points in the night sky, called *radiants*. Meteor showers are called *perseids* because their radiant is in the constellation Perseus.

A project for the young astronomer

One of the most relaxing activities for an observer is to simply count meteors. You can watch on any clear night, but it helps if the Moon is in a small phase, so it does not interfere with your observations.

Meteors are very diverse; they can appear to be of different colors and brightnesses. Many of the meteors we see are simple streaks of light. You can determine the magnitude of meteors by comparing their brightness to surrounding stars. Sometimes a meteor can become as bright as magnitude -10, almost as bright as the Full Moon. These meteors are called *fireballs*. Fireballs have, on occasion, exploded. Exploding fireballs, called *bolides*, often drop a trail of material along their path.

To observe either sporadic or shower meteors, all you need is a place to relax under the stars. Use a reclining chair and keep a pencil, paper, and charts handy. Try to plot the path of the meteors you see on the chart, especially if you are observing during a meteor shower. If you plot enough paths, you should be able to trace the meteors back to their radiant.

Glossary

absolute magnitude A measure of the luminosity of a star. The magnitude the star would have if it were 32.5 light-years (10 parsecs) from the Sun.

altitude The distance of an object above the horizon.

apparent magnitude The magnitude of a star or object as it appears to the unaided eye.

apparition The period of time when a celestial object is visible.

arcminute A unit of measure (') equal to 1/60 degree.

arcsecond A unit of measure (") equal to 1/3600 degree.

asterism An easily identifiable figure or shape formed by the stars of a constellation.

astronomical unit A unit for measuring distance equal to the average distance from the Earth to the Sun (93 million miles). Abbreviated AU.

azimuth A form of measurement running clockwise around the horizon from north (000), to east (090), south (180), and west (270).

celestial equator The line that is 90 degrees from the NCP and the SCP. The celestial equator is a projection of the Earth's equator into space.

celestial sphere An imaginary sphere surrounding Earth on which the stars appear to be placed.

constellation A group of stars that occupy a specific location in the sky.

declination A measure of the distance of an object, in degrees, north (+) or south (−) of the celestial equator. Abbreviated dec.

degree A unit of measure (°) equal to two Full-Moon diameters.

double star Two stars that appear close together in space. Double stars can be *binary doubles*, which are bound together by gravity and revolve around a common center of gravity, or *optical doubles*, which only appear to be double because they lie along our line of sight.

ecliptic   The apparent path of the Sun against the background stars.

focal length   The distance it takes an objective to form an image.

galaxy   A huge collection of stars, gas, and dust. Galaxies are found in three types: spiral, elliptical, and irregular. The Milky Way is a spiral galaxy.

H-R diagram   A graphic plot of stars that plots absolute magnitude vs. spectral magnitude.

horizon   The line where the sky and the earth meet.

kilo   A prefix meaning 1000.

light pollution   Stray light that leaks into the sky causing a loss of visibility of faint stars and objects.

light-year   The basic unit for measuring the universe equal to the distance light travels at 186,000 miles per second in one year. One light-year equals 5.6 trillion miles. Abbreviated ly.

limb   The edge of the Sun, Moon, or planet.

limiting magnitude   The faintest magnitude that can be seen; for the human eye, magnitude 6.5.

luminosity   The amount of energy given off as light by a star. Often compared to the luminosity of the Sun.

lunation   The period from one New Moon to the next New Moon.

mega   A prefix meaning 1 million.

meridian   An imaginary line drawn from the point on the horizon directly under Polaris (north), through the overhead point (zenith) and to the southernmost point of the horizon.

Messier Catalog   A listing of deep-sky objects developed by Charles Messier in the late 1700s. Each object in this catalog is assigned a number preceded by the letter *M*.

meteor   A meteroid that reaches the Earth's atmosphere but that burns up with the intense heat generated by its entry into our atmosphere. The result is a streak of light that crosses that sky. *Also called* a shooting star.

meteorite   A meteor that reaches the ground.

meteoroid   A small particle of material that travels through the Solar System.

nebula   A collection of dust or gas in space.

North Celestial Pole   The point at which the Earth's axis would intersect the celestial sphere if it were extended into space. Abbreviated NCP.

objective   The light-gathering portion of an optical instrument.

parsec A unit for measuring interstellar distances and equal to 3.2 light-years. Abbreviated pc.

right ascension Similar to longitude on Earth and measured eastward from the vernal equinox in hours, minutes, and seconds. Abbreviated RA.

sidereal Having to do with the stars. Sidereal time measures star time.

star cluster A group of stars bound together by gravity and traveling through space. *Open clusters* are groups of young stars found mainly in the spiral arms of our galaxy. *Globular clusters* are groups of much older stars that accompany the galaxy through space.

terminator The line that marks the division between the light and dark portion of a planet or moon.

transit The act of crossing the meridian drawn on the celestial sphere. When a star transits the meridian, it is at its highest point in the sky. *Also* called *culmination*.

transparency The clarity of the sky.

zenith The point exactly overhead on the celestial sphere.

zodiac The constellations that lie along the ecliptic.

Suggested reading

BOOKS

Abell, George O. *Exploration of the Universe*. New York: Holt, Reinhart & Winston, 1974. An excellent introductory text on astronomy.

Ashbrook, Joseph. *The Astronomical Scrapbook*. Cambridge, MA, Sky Publishing Corp, 1984. One of the best books on astro-history around. These articles originally appeared in *Sky & Telescope* magazine.

Asimov, Isaac. *Eyes on the Universe*. Boston: Houghton Mifflin, 1975. A well-written history of telescopes and the way we look at the sky.

Burnham, R.J. Jr. *Burnham's Celestial Handbook*. New York: Dover Publications, 1978. This three-volume set covers everything out there. An excellent, fun-to-read reference.

Cherrington, E.H. *Exploring the Moon Through Binoculars and a Small Telescope*. New York: Dover Publications, 1984. An excellent introduction to observing the Moon. It contains good photos, but the charts are a bit confusing.

Eicher, David. *The Universe from Your Backyard*. Milwaukee, WI: Astromedia, 1988. An excellent introduction to what's visible in each constellation.

Fulton, Ken. *The Light-Hearted Astronomer*. Milwaukee, WI: Astromedia, 1984. A light, easy-to-read account of what amateur astronomy is like. Excellent.

MacRobert, Alan. *Backyard Astronomy*. Cambridge, MA: Sky Publishing Corp., 1986.

_____. *More Backyard Astronomy*. Cambridge, MA: Sky Publishing Corp., 1989. These are good introductions to astronomy with some good pointers for the beginner.

Mallas, John & Kreimer, E. *The Messier Album*. Cambridge, MA: Sky Publishing Corp., 1978. An introduction to the Messier objects. This is a good introduction to deep-sky observing.

Mayall, R. & Mayall, M. *Olcott's Field Book of the Skies*; New York: G.P. Putnam's Sons, 1954. This may be old, but if you can find this book, grab it!

Norton, A.P. *Star Atlas and Reference Handbook*, 17th Edition. Essex, England: Longman Scientific & Technical, 1978. The classic star atlas, now in its ninetieth year in print.

Peltier, Leslie. *Starlight Nights.* Cambridge, MA: Sky Publishing Corp., 1965. One man's odyssey from rank beginner to world-class amateur. If you don't read anything else on this list, read this one!

Raymo, Chet. *365 Starry Nights.* Englewood Cliffs, NJ: Prentice-Hall, 1982. An easy-to-read introduction to astronomy.

Tirion, W. *Sky Atlas 2000.* Cambridge, MA: Sky Publishing Corp., 1981. The best star atlas for the beginner.

Webb, Rev. T.W. *Celestial Objects for Common Telescopes.* NY: Dover, 1963. A wonderful two-volume set (volume 1 is on the Solar System, volume 2 is on deep-sky objects). Originally written in the nineteenth century, it is a peek at how astronomers saw the sky over 100 years ago.

Whitney, Charles. *Whitney's Star Finder.* New York: Alfred A. Knopf, 1985. This classic introduction to the night sky includes a planisphere.

PERIODICALS, YEARLY BOOKS, ETC.

Sky & Telescope Magazine   Published monthly. Contains articles for all levels of amateur astronomy, although it can be a bit deep. Subscription runs $21.95 per year. Single-issue price $2.95.

Astronomy Magazine   Published monthly. Contains articles for all levels of amateur astronomy. This is a bit easier to understand than *Sky & Telescope*. Subscription runs $21.00 per year. Single-issue price $2.50.

Deep Sky Magazine   Published quarterly. Aimed at the amateur who concentrates on observing deep-sky objects. Subscription runs $12.00 per year. Single-issue price $3.00.

The Starry Messenger   Published monthly. Contains ads for astro-equipment for sale by amateurs around the country. Some great bargains. Subscription runs $18.00 per year.

The Observer's Handbook   Published yearly by the Royal Astronomical Society of Canada. Monthly listings of what's happening in the sky. Listings of solar, lunar, and planetary information. Price $10. Available at Adler Bookshop.

The Astronomical Calendar   Published yearly by Guy Ottewell. Monthly listing of sky events. Excellent graphics and explanatory text. Available from Sky Publishing, $14.00.

Index

A

absolute magnitude, 50, 133
Achernar, 10
Acrux, 10, 104
Adams, John C., 129
Albireo, 10
Alcor, 34
Aldebaran, 10, 39, 40, 42
Algol, 88, 94, 97, 98, 99, 100
Alpha Centauri, 18, 52, 64
Altair, 10, 18, 76, 81
altitude, 133
Alvan Clark & Sons, 50
Andromeda, 1, 7, 74, 87, 88, 90, 94
 M31 galaxy, 31-32, 60, 90-91
Andromeda galaxy, 31-32, 60, 90-91
Antares, 10, 68, 71
Antilia, 7, 64
Apis, 103
apparent magnitude, 50, 133
apparent motion, 11
apparition, 119, 133
Apus, 7, 102
Aquarius, 7, 57, 74, 87-89
Aquila, 7, 76, 81
Ara, 7, 103
Archernar, 52
Archimedes crater, 112

arcminute, 133
arcsecond, 133
Arcturus, 10, 17, 67, 68
Argo Navis, 53
Aries, 7, 57, 87, 88, 94
Aristarchus crater, 118
Aristotle crater, 112
asterisms, 1-6, 133
astronomical unit, 133
Astronomy magazine, 124, 128
atlases and maps, 25-28
atmospheric extinction, 65
Auriga, 7, 39, 40, 45-46, 74
Austin, Comet, 129
autumn constellations, 87-100
Ayades, 41
azimuth, 133

B

Bailly crater, Moon, 110
Barnard's Star, 18
Barnard, E.E., 81
Bayer, Johann, 9, 53, 101
Beehive cluster, 57
Bessel Crater, 112
Beta Cygni, 10
Betelgeuse, 10, 39, 40, 48

Big Dipper (*see also* Ursa Major), 4, 5, 34
binary doubles, 133
binary stars, eclipsing, 45
binoculars, 23-24
bolides, 132
Bootes, 7, 34, 67, 68
Bradfield Comet, 131
Brahe, Tycho, 21, 36
Bunsen, Robert W., 41

C

Caelum, 7, 53
Callisto, Jovian moon, 125
Camelopardalis, 7, 31, 34, 35
canals, Martian, 123
Cancer, 7, 37, 55-57, 74
Canes venatici, 7, 56, 58, 74
Canis Major, 1, 7, 40, 50-52, 74
Canis Minor, 1, 7, 40, 52
Canopus, 10
Capella, 10, 17, 39, 40, 45
Capricornus, 7, 57, 76, 81
captured rotation, Moon, 107
Carina, 7
Cassiopeia, 7, 31, 35, 36, 37, 87
Castor, 40, 48
celestial equator, 15, 133
celestial sphere, 15, 133
Centaurus, 7, 64, 68
Cepheus, 7, 31, 36-37, 87
   Cepheid variables, 37
   Delta Cephei, 36
Cetus, 1, 7, 87, 88, 91-94
Chamaeleon, 7, 104
Circinus, 7, 104
circumpolar constellations, 31-37
clusters, star, 42, 72, 96, 135
Columba, 7, 40, 53
Coma bernices, 7, 58
comets, 129
cones, human eye, 21
constellations, 1-5, 133
   circumpolar, 31-37, 31
   genitive or possessive case name, 9
   movement across sky, 11-16
   movement across sky, photo of, 13
   movement over time, 4-9, 14
   naming, 9-10
Copernicus crater, 117
Corona, 71
Corona australius, 7, 68
Corona borealis, 7, 68
Corvus, 7, 56, 62-64

Crab Nebula, 41-44
Crater, 7, 56, 62, 64
craters, Moon, 110
Crux, 7, 104
culmination, 135
Cygni 61, 18
Cygnus, 7, 74, 76-78, 81
   Deneb, 77
   North American Nebula, 78, 79

D

dark adaptation, night vision, 21-23
dark nebulae, 48, 81
Darquier, Antoine, 77
declination, 133
deep-sky objects, 45, 55
degrees, 15-16, 133
Delphinus, 7, 76, 81
Delta Cephei, 36
Deneb, 10, 76-78
distances, measurement of, 18-19
Dorado, 7, 104
Double Cluster, 96
double stars, 10, 34, 51-52, 133
   eclipsing binaries, 45, 97
   optical, 34, 35
   physical, 35
Draco, 7, 12, 31, 34-36
Dumbbell Nebula, 80

E

Earth
   dimensions of, 19
   distance to Moon, 19
earthshine, Moon, 109
eclipse, lunar, 18
eclipsing binary stars, 45, 97
ecliptic, 57, 119, 134
elliptical galaxy, 62
elongations, western and eastern, 119
emission nebulae, 48
Epsilon Aurigae, 45, 52
Epsilon Eridani, 18, 52
Equuleus, 7, 87, 88, 89
Eridanus, 7, 40, 52
Eta Cassiopeiae, 18
Eudoxus crater, 112
eyes and vision, seeing in the dark, 21-23

F

Fabricus, David, 91
fireballs, 132
first-magnitude stars, 16

Flamsteed numbers, 10
Flamsteed, John, 10
focal length, 24, 134
Formalhaut, 10, 88, 89
Fornax, 7, 87, 94

G

Galactic Center, 84
galactic clusters, 42
galaxy, 18, 42, 59, 60, 62, 90-91, 94, 95, 134
Galileo, ix, 24, 107, 125, 127
Galle, J.G., 129
Gemini, 7, 40, 48-50, 57, 74
genitive case, constellation name, 9
globular cluster, 55, 72, 135
Great Andromeda Galaxy, 90-91
Great Bear (see Ursa Major)
Great nebula, 48, 49
Great Square of Pegasus, 88, 97
Greek alphabet, 9
Grus, 7, 105

H

Hadar, 10
Hercules, 1, 2, 7, 10, 68, 72, 74
Herschel, William, 50, 55, 127
Hertzsprung, Ejar, 67, 69, 70
Hertzsprung-Russell Diagrams, 67, 69, 70, 134
highlands, lunar, 110-111
Hipparchus of Rhodes, 16, 17
horizon, 134
Horologium, 7, 105
Hubble, Edwin, 91
Hyades, 39, 42
Hydra, 8, 56, 58, 62, 64, 74
Hydrus, 8, 102

I

Indus, 8, 103
inferior planets, 119, 120, 122
integrated magnitude, 57
Intergalactic Wanderer, NGC 2419, 55
International Astronomical Union (IAU), 6
irregular galaxy, 62

J

Jupiter, 17, 52, 123, 125-127

K

Kepler crater, 118
Kepler's star, 36

Kepler, Johann, 21, 22, 36
kilo, 134
Kirchoff, Gustav, 41
Kohoutek, Comet, 129

L

LaCaille, Nicolas, 53, 101
Lacerta, 8, 87, 88, 89
Large Magellanic Cloud, 104
latitude, 12
Le Verrier, Urbain, 129
Leo, 2, 3, 8, 34, 56, 57, 58, 62, 64
Leo minor, 8, 56, 58
Lepus, 8, 40, 52
Libra, 8, 57, 68, 72
libration, Moon, 107, 109
light curve, variable stars, 92, 100
light pollution, 31, 33, 64, 134
light, speed of, 18
light-years, 18, 134
limb, 134
limiting magnitude, 134
Linne crater, 112
long-period variable stars, 92-94
Lowell, Percival, 123
luminosity, 37, 50, 134
lunar eclipse, 18
lunation, 134
Lupus, 8, 72
Lynx, 8, 55, 56
Lyra, x, 8, 12, 76-77
    Ring nebula, 77
    Vega, 75-77

M

M31 galaxy, 31-32, 60, 90-91
M33 spiral galaxy, 94, 95
M81 galaxy, 61
M92 globular cluster, 72
Magellanic Clouds, 62, 63, 104, 106
magnitude, 16-17, 50
    absolute, 50, 133
    apparent, 50, 133
    Hertzsprung-Russell Diagrams, 67, 69, 70
    integrated, 57
    limiting, 134
main-sequence stars, 69
Manilius crater, 112
maps and atlases, 25-28
Mare Crisium, 112
Mare Fecunditatis, 112
Mare Imbrium, 112
Mare Nectaris, 112
Mare Serenitatis, 110

Mare Tranquillitatis, 112
Mare Vaporum, 112
maria, lunar seas, 110
Mars, 123-125
maxima, 92
mega, 134
Mensa, 8, 103
Mercury, 119-121, 123
meridian, 134
Messier Catalog, 44-45, 134
Messier, charles, 44, 77
meteor showers, 131
meteorites, 129, 134
meteoroids, 129, 134
meteors, 129, 134
Microscopium, 8, 103
Milky Way, 18, 55, 60, 81, 84, 85, 91, 104
Mimosa, 10
minima, 92
Mira, 10, 88, 91-94
Mizar, 34
Monoceros, 8, 40, 53, 74
Moon, x, 15, 17, 19, 107-118
    captured rotation, 107
    craters and seas on, 110
    earthshine, 109
    libration, 107, 109
    phases of, 107-109, 113-116
    ray systems of, 117
    sidereal period, 107
    terminator, 109
motion, apparent, 11
Musca, 8, 103

N

nebulae, 48, 77, 78, 79, 80, 81, 91, 134
Neptune, 50, 128-129
Newton, Isaac, 25, 39
Newtonian telescopes, 25
NGC 2419, deep-sky object, 55
night vision, 21-23
Norma, 8, 103
North American Nebula, 78, 79
North Celestial Pole, 11, 31, 34, 134
Norton's Star Atlas, 28, 85, 125
notebook for observations, 29-30
nova, 36, 44

O

objective, 24, 134
observation notebook, 29-30
Oceanus Procellarum, 112
Octans, 8, 103

Omicron Ceti, 10
Omicron-2 Eridani, 18
open clusters, 42, 96, 135
Ophiuchi 70, 18
Ophiuchus, 8, 68, 72-73
optical double stars, 34, 133
Orion, x, 1, 8, 37, 39, 40, 46-48, 49, 52

P

parallax, 19
parsec, 135
Pavo, 8, 105
Pegasus, 8, 74, 87, 88, 90, 97
Peiresc, Nicholas, 48
period, variable stars, 92
perseids, 132
Perseus, 1, 2, 3, 8, 9, 74, 87, 88, 94-97
    Double Cluster, 96
    meteor shower from, 132
phases, inferior planets, 122
phases, Moon, 107-109, 113-116
Phoenix, 8, 105
photoelectric photometers, star magnitude from, 17
physical double stars, 35
Picard, 112
Pickering, Edward, 41
Pictor, 8, 105
Pisces, 8, 37, 57, 87, 88, 98
Pisces Austrialis, 8, 87, 88, 89
planetary motion, laws of, 21, 22
planets (see solar system)
planisphere, 28, 29
Plato crater, 112
Pleiades, 41, 42, 43
Pluto, 25, 50, 123, 129-130
Polaris, 10-14, 31, 34
Pollux, 10, 40, 48
possessive case, constellation name, 9
Praesepe cluster, 57
precession, 11, 14
prism, light and, 41
Procyon, 10, 40, 52
proper motion, 5
protostars, 48
Pup, 50, 51
pupil, human eye, 21
Puppis, 8, 53, 74
Pyxis, 8, 64

R

radiants, 132
ray systems, Moon, 117

reflection nebulae, 48
reflector telescopes, 24, 25, 27
refractor telescopes, 24, 25, 26
Regulus, 10, 34, 56, 58, 64
Reticulum, 8, 105
retina, human eye, 21
retrograde motion, 123, 126
Riccioli, Giovanni, 34
Rigel, 10, 39, 48, 50, 52
Rigel Kent, 10
right ascension, 135
Ring Nebula, 77, 78
rods, human eye, 21
Russell, Henry, 67, 69, 70

S

Sagitta, 8, 76, 81
Sagittarius, 8, 57, 74, 76, 81
Saturn, 127-128
Schiaparelli, Giovanni, 123
Schmidt Cassegrain telescopes, 25, 27
Scorpius, 8, 57, 68, 71, 74
Sculptor, 8, 87, 90
Scutum, 8, 74, 76, 81
seas, Moon, 110
second-magnitude stars, 16
Serpens, 8, 68, 72-74
Sextans, 8, 58
Shapely, Harlow, 55
sidereal, 135
sidereal period, Moon, 107
Sidereus Nuncius, 107
Sirius, 10, 17, 18, 40, 51, 52
Sky & Telescope magazine, 98, 124, 127, 128
Sky Atlas 2000.0, 85, 125
Small Magellanic Cloud, 106
solar system, 119-132
    apparition, 119
    comets, 129
    inferior and superior planets, 119, 120, 122
    Jupiter, 125-127
    Mars, 123-125
    Mercury, 119-121
    meteors, 129
    Neptune, 128-129
    Pluto, 129-130
    retrograde motions, 123, 126
    Saturn, 127-128
    Uranus, 127-128
    Venus, 121-123
southern constellations, 101-106
spectral classes, stars, 41-42, 53-54

spectroscope, star colors, 39
Spica, 10, 17, 34, 56, 59
spiral galaxy, 60, 94, 95
sporadic meteors, 131
spring constellations, 55-65
star atlas, 28
star clusters, 42, 135
stars
    birth of, nebulae, 48
    brightness of, 50
    brightness of, magnitudes, 16-17
    brightness, Greek alphabet for, 9-10
    brightness, list of, 10
    colors of, 39-42, 53-54
    death of, 77
    distance to, 18
    double, 10, 34, 35, 51-52, 97
    integrated magnitude, 57
    luminosity, 37
    luminosity of, 50
    main-sequence, 69
    Messier Catalog of, 44-45
    naming, Greek alphabet for, 9-10
    numbering of, Flamsteed numbers, 10
    optical double, 34, 35
    physical double, 35
    spectral classes, 41-42, 53-54
    types of, 39-42
    variable, 10, 36, 37, 45, 92-94
    white-dwarf, 52, 105
summer constellations, 67-85
Sun, 17, 18, 19
superior planets, 119, 120, 122
supernova, 36, 44, 105

T

Tau Cetia, 18
Taurus, 2, 8, 39-45, 47, 48, 57, 74
    Aldebaran, 39, 42
    Ayades, 41
    Crab Nebula, 41-44
    Hyades, 39, 42
    Pleiades, 41, 42
telescopes, 24-25
    focal length, 24
    Newtonians, 25
    objectives, 24
    reflector, 24, 25, 27
    refractors, 24, 25, 26
    Schmidt Cassegrain, 25, 27
Telescopium, 8, 106
terminator, Moon, 109, 135
Theophilus crater, 112

third-magnitude stars, 16
Thuban, 14
time-exposure photograph, star
    movement, 13
Tirion, Wil, 85
Tombaugh, Clyde, 25, 50, 130
transit, 135
transparency, 135
Triangulum, 8, 74, 87, 88, 94, 95
Triangulum australe, 8, 106
Tucana, 8, 106
Tycho crater, 117
Tycho's star, 36
Type I supernovae, 105
Type II supernovae, 105

U

Universal Time, 98
Uranometria, 101
Uranus, 50, 127-129
Ursa Major, x, 4, 5, 8, 32-34, 37
    Big Dipper, 34
    M81 galaxy in, 61
    Mizar, 34

Polaris, 34
Ursa Minor, 8, 10, 11, 31, 34-35

V

variable stars, 10, 36, 37, 45, 98
    long-period, 92-94
Vega, 10, 12, 14, 17, 75-77
Vela, 9, 106
Venus, x, 17, 121-123
Virgo, 9, 34, 56, 57, 59-62
    Galaxy Cluster in, 59
    M87, elliptical galaxy, 62
Volans, 9, 106
von Fraunhofer, Joseph, 39, 41
Vulpecula, 9, 37, 76, 78, 80

W

white dwarf stars, 52, 105
white nebulae, 91
winter constellations, 39-54

Z

zenith, 135
zodiac, 55, 57, 135

Other Bestsellers of Related Interest

PUZZLES, PARADOXES, AND BRAIN TEASERS—*Stan Gibilisco*

Explore the loopholes in mathematical logic! This is a clear, concise, well-written exploration of the mysteries of the universe. It is an intriguing look at those exceptions that are as frustrating as they are amusing. The author's approach is entertaining, enlightening, and easy to understand. Although the topics are of a mathematical nature, the discussions are nontechnical. 122 pages, 83 illustrations. **Book No. 2895, $8.95 paperback only**

REACHING FOR INFINITY: Puzzles, Paradoxes and Brainteasers #3—*Stan Gibilisco*

Explore the infinite with Stan Gibilisco in his third *Puzzles, Paradoxes, and Brainteasers* book. This collection of nontechnical mind exercises will arouse your curiosity. Gibilisco shows you the physical nature of infinity and leads you to examine infinity of space and time, particles, numbers, arithmetic, visualizing infinity, and geometric infinities. You'll explore the physical nature of infinity in the hierarchy of particles and number theory. 140 pages, 67 illustrations. **Book No. 3327, $16.95 hardcover, $9.95 paperback**

SCIENCE FAIR: Developing a Successful and Fun Project—*Maxine Haren Iritz,*
Photographs by A. Frank Iritz

Here's all the step-by-step guidance parents and teachers need to help students complete prize-quality science fair projects! This book provides easy-to-follow advice on every step of science fair project preparation from choosing a topic and defining the problem to conducting the experiment, drawing conclusions, and setting up the fair display. 96 pages, 83 illustrations. **Book No. 2936, $16.95 hardcover, $9.95 paperback**

LIGHT, LASERS, AND OPTICS—*John H. Mauldin*

A fascinating introduction to the science and technology of modem optics. Broad enough to appeal to the general science enthusiast, yet technically specific enough for the experienced electronics hobbyist, this book fully explains the science of optics. You'll explore: everyday observations on light, the theory and physics of light and atoms, computing with light, optical information storage, and many other related subjects! *Light, Lasers, and Optics* is extremely well illustrated with over 200 line drawings. 240 pages, 205 illustrations. **Book No. 3038, $14.95 paperback only**

333 *MORE* SCIENCE TRICKS AND EXPERIMENTS—*Robert J. Brown*

Now, a second big collection of science "tricks" and demonstrations from the author of the popular syndicated newspaper column, *Science and You!* Designed to make learning basic scientific principles exciting and fun, this is an ideal sourcebook for parents, teachers, club and scout leaders . . . and just about anyone who's fascinated with the wonders of scientific and natural phenomena! 240 pages, 213 illustrations. **Book No. 1835, $16.95 hardcover, $10.95 paperback**

HOMEMADE HOLOGRAMS: The Complete Guide to Inexpensive, Do-It-Yourself Holography—*John Iovine*

Make your own holograms, easily and inexpensively with this breakthrough book. John Iovine tells you how to produce laser-generated images plus equipment like a portable isolation table and a helium-neon laser. You'll also construct devices that can make your experiments easier and more professional, such as magnetic film holders, spatial filters, an electronic shutter, an audible electronic timer, and a laser power meter and photometer. 208 pages, 185 illustrations. **Book No. 3460, $22.95 hardcover, $14.95 paperback**

EXPLORING EARTH FROM SPACE—*Jon Erickson*

Learn how orbiting satellites are used to explore our planet. Geophysicist Jon Erickson covers the technology—how satellite images are collected and processed—and describes how this technology is applied in weather forecasting, land-use planning, geologic mapping, mineral exploration, agriculture, disaster control and more. 207 pages, 157 illustrations. **Book No. 3242, $23.95 hardcover, $15.95 paperback**

STUDIES IN STARLIGHT: Understanding Our Universe—*Charles J. Caes*

Even those with only limited exposure to electromagnetic concepts will find this book engrossing and understandable. Pictures and prose relate the histories of efforts made to understand the mysteries of our universe by ancient, medieval, and modern civilizations. Caes tells a tate that inspires wonder, validates theories, and dispels myths. 240 pages, 77 illustrations. **Book No. 2946, $12.95 paperback only**

THROUGH THE TELESCOPE: A Guide for the Amateur Astronomer—*Michael R. Porcellino*

Through the Telescope is an open invitation to explore our universe. This book and an amateur astronomical telescope are all you need to meet the multitude of stars, nebulae, and deep-sky objects that can be seen on a dark, clear night. Porcellino guides you on a tour of the Moon, where you'll visit craters, mountains, and rilles, and learn to identify them by their unique features. Next you'll move out to the satellites of Jupiter, the rings of Saturn, and even the Sun. 352 pages, 217 illustrations. **Book No. 3159, $26.95 hardcover, $18.95 paperback**

THE MYSTERIOUS OCEANS—*Jon Erickson*

Explores far below the foamy crest and delve into the wonders of the sea—its forces, its predators, its role in the food chain, its mountains, and much more. The author covers topics of oceanography, geology, meteorology, and marine biology. 208 pages, 169 illustrations. **Book No. 3042, $22.95 hardcover, $14.95 paperback**

Prices Subject to Change Without Notice.

Look for These and Other TAB Books at Your Local Bookstore

To Order Call Toll Free 1-800-822-8158

(in PA, AK, and Canada call 717-794-2191)

or write to TAB BOOKS, Blue Ridge Summit, PA 17294-0840.

Title		Product No.	Quantity	Price

☐ Check or money order made payable to TAB BOOKS

Charge my ☐ VISA ☐ MasterCard ☐ American Express

Acct. No. _____ Exp. _____

Signature: _____

Name: _____

Address: _____

City: _____

State: _____ Zip: _____

Subtotal $ _____

Postage and Handling
($3.00 in U.S., $5.00 outside U.S.) $ _____

Add applicable state and local
sales tax $ _____

TOTAL $ _____

TAB BOOKS catalog free with purchase; otherwise send $1.00 in check or money order and receive $1.00 credit on your next purchase.

Orders outside U.S. must pay with international money order in U.S. dollars.

TAB Guarantee: If for any reason you are not satisfied with the book(s) you order, simply return it (them) within 15 days and receive a full refund. **BC**